Handcrafted Christmas

Handcrafted Christmas

Ornaments, Decorations, and Cookie Recipes to Make at Home

• •

By Susan Waggoner

Photographs by Dane Holweger

Stewart, Tabori & Chang | New York

Published in 2014 by Stewart, Tabori & Chang
An imprint of ABRAMS

Library of Congress Control Number: 2014930833
ISBN: 978-1-61769-056-3

Editor: Dervla Kelly
Designer: Kay Schuckhart/Blond on Pond
Production Manager: Erin Vandeveer
Photography Direction & Production: Karen Schaupeter Creative
Photographer: Dane Holweger
Digital Tech: Chris Nowling
Prop Styling: Lauren Machen

The text of this book was composed in Adobe Caslon.

Printed and bound in the United States
10 9 8 7 6 5 4 3 2 1

Stewart, Tabori & Chang books are available at special discounts when purchased in quantity for
premiums and promotions as well as fundraising or educational use. Special editions can also be created to
specification. For details, contact specialsales@abramsbooks.com or the address below.

THE ART OF BOOKS SINCE 1949

115 West 18th Street
New York, NY 10011
www.abramsbooks.com

CONTENTS

The Meaning of Handcrafted

I was lucky enough to grow up in a family of crafters. On my father's side, the men built things. My grandmother, aunts, and even my busy mother took classes in whatever skill was on offer—enameled jewelry, Japanese flower arranging, interior design, and a strange 1950s craft where you drilled a three-dimensional flower into the backside of a Lucite or resin block, painted the hollowed-out parts, and ended up with what, turned right side up, appeared to be a blossom floating in a block of ice. If anyone knows what that was called, I would love to know.

On my mother's side, my Swedish grandmother was so accomplished with a crochet hook she could have made lace of plain sewing thread if asked. Our birthdays always brought embroidered sheets and pillowcases edged with delicate crochet, undervalued and taken for granted then—now among my most treasured possessions.

Christmas, of course, was the highlight of the crafting year. Sequins and glitter flew like a multicolored blizzard. Fabric was cut, paint sets were purchased. One year my mother made and costumed a choir and orchestra of heavenly angels, each holding sheet music or a miniature instrument. They hovered above our fireplace around a fairly grand pipe organ my father made from black lacquered wood and tiers of pencils spray-painted gold. The next year, we spent several Saturdays helping an aunt cover sections of cardboard tubes with white felt and gold ribbon to make small drums. She didn't tell us what they were for, but when we arrived for Christmas Eve, there was a magnificent white flocked tree, the first I'd ever seen, adorned with small white bears in red British jackets, each playing a drum. That was the same year my grandmother, born on an Iowa farm in 1886, surprised us all with marzipan fruit fit for a Fortnum & Mason display table.

The value and meaning of "handcrafted" has changed often throughout history. During hard times, handcrafted items serve as stand-ins for gifts one can't afford to buy. Or, with the help of a purchased pattern, they become the solution when the toy shelves are picked clean. In better times, handcrafted means someone cared enough to spend time rather than money to provide something uniquely created, something that could not be bought.

If you're a crafter, you have no doubt had the experience of someone telling you, "You could make those to sell." But, of course, you don't make them to sell. These items can only be made to share with people you love. If I had my way, every Christmas would be a handcrafted one.

A WORD OF WARNING

A few of the projects in this book call for Twinklets Diamond Dust, an old-fashioned glass glitter which is beautiful but highly dangerous to pets and children. Glitter has a way of scattering about while you're working, and when animals pick it up on their paws and fur, or children get the lovely, candy-colored stuff on their fingers, there's a tendency to lick it off and—well, it's ground glass. When crafting with pets or children in the house, substitute kosher or epsom salt, or modern glitter which is made of small plastic particles and is, by and large, gorgeous. The trade is a small price to pay, and we don't want anyone injured through an excess of vintage spirit.

The Projects

LITTLE VILLAGE HOUSE

The tradition of setting out small houses and village scenes at Christmas derives from the custom of displaying nativity scenes in front of churches, a practice introduced by St. Francis in 1223. By casting living people and animals in the dramatic Biblical scene, St. Francis hoped to remind worshippers that Christmas was more about the birth of Christ than it was about gifts and revelry.

Within a few centuries, statues replaced living actors, and the scenes grew larger and more elaborate. Royal courts and the very wealthy collected figures for their own scenes. For ordinary folk, small wooden figures or inexpensive ones made from clay made it possible to enjoy miniature scenes at home. Of the many traditions associated with nativity displays, one of the oddest was the British custom of baking the Christmas dinner minced pie in the shape of a manger, in which the figure of the Holy Infant rested until it was time to serve the pie. Among the many yuletide festivities the Puritans banned, the minced pie merited special attention; it was outlawed as "idolatry in a crust."

The Moravians in particular established a tradition of arranging small nativity scenes beneath their Christmas trees. When they came to America and settled in Pennsylvania and North Carolina, they brought their tradition with them. Over the years, the scenes became more secular. By the late nineteenth century, small villages and farmlands, composed of the children's toys, were more common than nativity scenes beneath the tree. In the 1930s, Germany produced mass numbers of small cardboard pieces for export to the United States. Known as *putz*, or glitter houses, the pieces were varied and elaborate. In addition to homes, there

were churches scaled to match, and whole villages could be created and adorned with drifts of cotton snow and small bottlebrush trees. Japan also made putz houses, especially after World War II, but in general theirs were not as elaborate as the prewar German structures had been and were often smaller and meant to be hung as ornaments rather than displayed as part of a street scene. Today, Christmas villages are usually made of ceramic and collected piece by piece. We think it's fun to make our own, and the ways to alter a single pattern and the finishing process ensure plenty of variety.

MATERIALS

Tracing paper

Pencil

Lightweight cardboard, such as from cereal or cracker boxes

Ruler, preferably a clear, graphed one

Craft knife or scissors

Contrasting-color cardstock, such as light blue, for the door

White cardstock or index cards for window frames and door frame

Dry embossing tool

Craft mat

Scotch Positionable Mounting Adhesive

Brayer or rolling pin

Clean, unused printer paper

Glitter, your choice of colors

Bone folder or table knife

White acrylic craft paint

Paintbrush

Duct tape

Mod Podge

Paper towel tube or toilet paper tube (optional)

Bamboo skewer

E6000 glue

Twinklets Diamond Dust

Length of green tinsel craft stem

Red Stickles Glitter Glue

Use tracing paper to copy all the patterns on page 139. Include the lines for the door and windows on the sloped piece, which will be the front and the back of the house. Cut out the traced patterns.

Flip the sloped piece over, so the swoop is on the right when the pattern faces you. Lay the pattern on the unprinted side of a piece of cardboard. Trace and cut out. This will be the back of the house, so you don't need to mark the door or windows.

Flip the pattern right side up, with the swoop on the left. Trace the outline onto the unprinted side of a piece of cardboard and cut out. Trace the door. Make a dot in all four corners of each window. Set the pattern aside and use a ruler to connect the dots in each window. Check measurements against the side and bottom of the house to make sure the windows are straight. If not, redraw to make the adjustment. You are going to cover this side with glitter, so your lines won't show. Cut out the door and windows.

To make the door, place the contrasting cardstock (light blue on our house) under the front piece of the house and, with bottom edges even, trace the inside of the cut-out door onto the cardstock. Do the same with a piece of white cardstock. On the white piece, make a series of small marks all the way around the door, measuring about ¼ inch (6 mm) out. Connect the dots to sketch a larger version of the blue door. Cut out the pieces (using the larger outline as your cut line on the white cardstock) and set aside.

Trace and cut out the two side pieces. Draw the windows as described above and cut out the spaces.

On another piece of cardboard, draw and cut out a rectangle that measures 4½ by 7 inches (11 by 18 cm). This will be the roof. Turn it over so the printed side is up. On the long side, measure off 4 inches (10 cm) and make a mark near the edge. Do the same on the edge directly across from the first mark. Draw a line connecting the two marks, so the piece is divided into a 4-inch (10-cm) section and a 3-inch (7.5-cm) section. Position your ruler edge on the line and run the bone folder along it to make an indented line.

The next step is to apply glitter to the four sides of the house. Place one of the pieces, unprinted side up, on a clean, washable surface, such as a craft mat. Cut a piece of mounting adhesive large enough to cover the piece. Position it over the piece with the exposed sticky side down and the protective liner up. Press firmly over the adhesive, smoothing with your hands. It's important to get good and complete coverage, so go over the surface with a brayer or rolling pin.

When you are satisfied that the adhesive is firmly in place, use a craft knife or scissors to trim off the excess liner. Cut away adhesive from the doors and windows.

Peel away the covering and lay the piece, sticky side up, on the printer paper. Cover liberally with glitter. Cover with a second sheet of paper and press down with your hands, a brayer, or a rolling pin to really push the glitter into the sticky adhesive. Let set a few minutes, then pick up the piece by the edge, shake off excess glitter, and set aside to finish curing. Return unused glitter to the container.

Cover the remaining three sides of the house with glitter in the same way. Let cure a few hours.

Meanwhile, make the roof. Fold the printed sides of the cardboard together along the indented line to make a peaked tent with one side longer than the other. Go over the crease with a bone folder or the handle of a table knife to make a sharp crease. Paint the surface of the roof white, starting at the top along the crease and making brush strokes down to the eaves. Allow to dry, then turn the roof over and paint a border on the underside, from each edge to about ¾ inch (2 cm) in. Let dry. Apply a second coat if needed and set aside to dry completely.

To join the walls together, you'll need duct tape. Lay the front of the house and one of the side walls face down on a clean surface. Push them together face down so the edges of the walls meet perfectly. Make sure the bottom edges are perfectly aligned. Cut a length of duct tape the height of the joining walls and adhere it, lengthwise, over the place where the walls join. Press the tape firmly to get a good, tight join. It doesn't matter if there are a few wrinkles in the tape; just press them flat with your fingertips. When you pick up the joined pieces, you'll see that you've formed a hinge.

Lay the joined pieces flat again and join the other side wall to the front of the house in the same way.

With the joined pieces flat, join the side wall nearest to the swoop to the back of the house on the side with the swoop.

To make the final join, lay the back of the house, glitter side down, on a flat surface. Run a length of duct tape down along the unattached edge of the back wall, leaving half of the tape free to attach to the side wall. Then, with your other hand bracing the side wall and pushing the two edges close, adhere the free edge of the tape to the inside of the side wall.

If the outside corners where the walls join look a bit rough or expose any cardboard, use a small brush to paint the area with Mod Podge and sprinkle on more glitter. Mod Podge dries clear, so it won't matter if you get some on an area that is already covered with glitter.

While touch-ups are drying, prepare the roof. Our roof obligingly curled on the side that will cover the swoop. If yours didn't, roll the end halfway around a paper towel tube or toilet paper tube for a few minutes to encourage a curl.

Use a bamboo skewer to apply a line of E6000 glue to the top edges of all four sides of the house, wherever the roof will touch. Position the roof and hold it in place until it sticks. This is a temporary bond, so cut tabs of duct tape and join the roof to the house as you joined the walls on the inside of the house. Four tabs on a side will do it.

Paint the roof with Mod Podge and liberally sprinkle with Diamond Dust.

To make the window frames, use white cardstock or index cards. For the four side windows, draw four 1-inch (2.5-cm) squares on the wrong side of the cardstock. Measure and draw a line a little less than ¼ inch (6 mm) in on all four sides. Cut out the frames.

To make the lower front window, draw a 1-by-2-inch (2.5-by-5-cm) rectangle. Again, measure and draw a line a little less than ¼ inch (6 mm) in on all four sides.

Cut out the frame. Make the upper window in the same way, starting with a rectangle that measures 1 by ¾ inch (2.5 by 2 cm).

Use a bamboo skewer to dab E6000 glue around a window, then attach the frame. Finish each window this way.

Dab a bit of E6000 glue onto the back of the smaller door and attach it to the larger door. Use a bamboo skewer to dab E6000 glue on the front of the house around the edge of the cutout door and attach the door over it.

For the finishing touch, make a wreath by winding a section of a green tinsel craft stem around the barrel of a pen. Twist the two ends together and trim off excess craft stem. Use red Glitter Glue to make clusters of holly berries. You might want to practice first, as it takes just a tiny drop to make a berry. Set the wreath aside for a day to let the Glitter Glue dry completely.

You're ready to move in!

VARIATIONS

You can make variations of this house by flipping the front and back pieces to make the swoop on the opposite side. You can make a symmetrical house by drawing a line from the peak at the top of the house straight down, folding your tracing paper in half, placing the fold along the line, and tracing just half of the house. Tracing the side with the swoop makes a good barn. Tracing the straight side will create a tidy little cottage. You can vary this little cottage by turning it to make the side the front, giving you a house with a hip roof, and moving the doors and windows accordingly. If you add 5 inches (12 cm) to the height of the hip roof house, you have a good structure for an apartment building or grand emporium.

CHRISTMAS CORSAGES

The idea of special Christmas jewelry and adornments dates back to the Victorian era, but post–World War II era United States put the custom on steroids. During the war, families separated by distance and danger resolved never to take another Christmas for granted, so post-war Christmases were filled with a joy that was almost uncontainable. Thanks to an economic boom, people actually had money to spend for the first time since the Depression. Not only did they feel joyous, but they could also now dress the part.

Women who had suffered through fabric shortages and clothes rationing during the war were especially delighted in being able to buy new items again. They wore nylons, glittered their hair for Christmas parties, and floated through the holidays in Dior's luxuriously full New Look skirts. From Thanksgiving to New Year's, Christmas corsages blossomed on the lapels of coats and suit jackets. It was as if every woman in the country was going to the prom, which was exactly the impression the style was meant to convey. There was even a classic pin-on for children that wasn't a floral piece, but rather a chunky plastic replica of Santa's head and shoulders, with red string and a jingle bell that hung from the center. When the string was pulled, Santa's red nose lit up. Corsages remained popular into the 1960s, and gradually became a kind of kitsch send-up of themselves, still fun but no longer elegant. We're all for bringing back their glory days.

Very lightweight wire, such as twist-tie wire with the plastic stripped off

Jewelry clippers or kitchen shears

E6000 glue

1 pin back for each corsage

FOR THE HOLLY LEAF CORSAGE

2 picks of green velvet holly leaves with berries, each with 3 leaves

Santa jingle bell or other charm

Jewelry head pin (optional)

3 red double-tipped berries

FOR THE BLUE LEAF AND BELLS CORSAGE

4 small plastic silver bells

Red nail polish

Mod Podge

Small paintbrush

Twinklets Diamond Dust

Several red double-tipped small stamens

Two 2-inch (5-cm) pale blue velvet millinery leaves on stems

Four 1½-inch (4-cm) pale blue velvet millinery leaves on stems

Two 2-inch (5-cm) cream velvet millinery leaves on stems

Four 1½-inch (4-cm) cream velvet millinery leaves on stems

Four 6-mm size round red glass beads

HOW-TO
HOLLY LEAF CORSAGE

Twist the 2 stems of the holly picks together.

Fan and bend the leaves to make a pleasing shape, with some of the leaves more prominent and some partly tucked behind to give the corsage depth. Remember, the leaves will be pointing up.

Thread the lightweight wire through the loop on the charm. Center the charm on the wire and twist the wire ends together near the loop of the charm. If you are using a charm without a loop, thread it onto a jewelry head pin, use round-nosed jewelry pliers to make a loop, wrap the head pin once around the base of the loop, and snip off the excess. Thread with wire as described above.

Adjust the height of your charm and secure in place by wrapping the wire several times around the holly cluster where the stems join.

Fold the twisted holly stems up behind the corsage, making a little loop where the stems and leaves begin. Twist the loop to make a tight bundle and trim off the excess wire.

Attach the red double-tipped berries by wrapping around the stems and arranging them to cover the knot.

Use E6000 glue to attach the pin back near the base of the corsage. Adjust the berries to hide any glints of metal that show.

BLUE LEAF AND BELLS CORSAGE

Paint 2 bells with red nail polish and set aside to dry.

Paint the remaining 2 bells with Mod Podge and sprinkle liberally with Diamond Dust.

When the bells are dry, fold a red double-tipped stamen in half unevenly, so the red tips are at slightly different levels. Dab a bit of E6000 glue around the fold and attach the stamen to the inside of a bell, making sure the red tips stick out of the bell. Repeat with each bell.

Thread the wire through the loop at the top of each bell. Center the bell on the wire, twist the wire ends together near the loop on the bell, and set aside.

Lay out the leaves in an arrangement that is appealing to you. Layer with the larger leaves to the back, building with the smaller leaves on top of them, and mix the colors for even balance. This is a free-form exercise, and you will make changes and adjustments as you go. You can twist the stems of two or three leaves together, poke in an extra leaf where it's needed and twisting its stem around another leaf, or any other method that works for you. We found it was easier to control the leaves and keep them where we wanted by having each stem twisted around at least one other stem.

As you work, you will also want to incorporate bundles of red stamens. Fold 2 or 3 stamens in half, staggering them at different lengths. Thread a length of wire through the loops, then wrap around the bundle, making sure you have a few inches of free wire left. Slide the bundle between the leaves so only the red tips show, and anchor by wrapping the ends of the wire around a leaf stem.

Thread a red glass bead onto the doubled wire of each bell. Anchor each bell separately near the center of the corsage. Holding the bell where you want it, pull the wire ends through to the back, leaving a bit of slack. Anchor the bell by wrapping the wire firmly several times around a stem. Repeat with each bell.

Adjust the leaves and bells as needed, and tuck in more stamen bundles if desired. When you're satisfied, twist the main stems tightly together at the back of the corsage. Fold the twisted stems down to make a curl hidden by the leaves.

Use E6000 glue to attach the pin back to the back of the corsage.

NEEDLE-FELTED SNOWMAN

Felt was the first fabric produced by man, dating back more than eight thousand years. Because the materials were inexpensive, lightweight, super-insulating, and far easier to work with than pelts, felt was especially prized in cold-climate regions like Lapland and Siberia, and the nomadic Mongols used it to make everything from boots to yurts. Felt lends itself well to embellishment, and over the centuries the artisans who made necessities from it also decorated their pieces with beautiful and distinctive designs. With the coming of spinning and weaving, and later industrialized fabric production, felting lost its dominance in much of the world. Felt was commercially produced largely for manufacturers, while small amounts were made for home crafters.

Felt is made by locking fleece fibers from sheep or other animals together, either by a wet soap-and-water process or by a dry process using specialized needles. The dry technique of needle felting was not initially embraced in the United States, and was largely unheard of until Eleanor Stanwood and her husband revived it as a way of making use of the fleece that many small sheep ranchers discarded. After first producing material for manufacturers to use as batting, they explored the artistic potential of the craft, making beautifully decorated comforters then moving to one-of-a-kind scarves and finally teaching other fabric artists their techniques. Felting began to build in popularity in the 1980s and today is a rapidly growing favorite with crafters. Wisconsin felting artist Barbara Voss designed this snowman to convince us that anyone can produce something wonderful on the first try. She was right!

Two 2-inch (5-cm) Styrofoam balls

Paring knife

E6000 glue

Dark green craft paint

Paintbrush

¼ ounce (7 g) (or less) white Corriedale (or Merino) wool roving

One 2½-inch (6-cm) Styrofoam ball

Pack of felting needles, 36 and 38 gauge, triangular

¼ ounce (7 g) (or less) dark-green Corriedale (or Merino) wool roving

Safety glasses

Jewelry clippers

Three 2-inch (5-cm) head pins

Bamboo skewer

A dab each of red and black Corriedale (or Merino) wool roving. (You can often find starter kits in crafts stores that give you some of each of all 4 wools needed, needles, and a foam mat.)

One 2-inch (5-cm) piece of black 6-strand embroidery thread (optional)

One 2-inch (5-cm) thick foam mat or two foam kitchen sponges, glued one on top of the other

Straight pins

One or two 12-inch (30.5-cm) chenille craft stems, your choice of colors

1 bottlebrush tree, 2½ to 3 inches (6 to 7.5 cm) long

HOW-TO

To make the feet, cut one of the 2-inch (5-cm) Styrofoam balls in half with a paring knife. With the cut side down, trim about ½ inch (12 mm) off one side of each ball. Glue the trimmed sides together with E6000 glue to form the boots. Allow to dry, then paint with dark green paint. Let dry, then paint the bottom of the boots as well and set aside to dry.

Now it's time to felt. If your wool roving arrived densely packed, pull the fibers apart as you work with it. Your wool should be light, cloudlike, and wispy—not thick and spongy. Lay a small piece (a bit more than 1 square inch [2.5 cm]) of white wool roving on the surface the 2½-inch (6-cm) Styrofoam ball. You are going to lightly tack it to the ball with a series of quick, straight, up-and-down jabs with the felting needle. Jab just far enough into the ball to hold the wool, and use just enough wool to cover. You are not trying to build up layers or create shapes, so don't place your jabs too close together. You are just giving the body a nice, fuzzy covering. You cannot make a mistake here—if you pack on too much wool and it looks too solid or dimply, just rip it off and start again. After you've attached the first piece, lay a second one beside it and repeat the process. Keep going until the entire ball is covered. Repeat the process to felt the head with white wool and the remaining 2-inch (5-cm) Styrofoam ball and the boots with the dark-green wool.

As you work, be careful not to jab your fingers. Felting needles have barbs that cause the fibers to interlock. If you jab your finger, those barbs hurt when you pull the needle out. Also, don't be alarmed if your needle breaks. This happens frequently, and it doesn't mean you're doing anything wrong. Just pick up a new needle and keep going.

When you finish felting, put on your safety glasses and use the jewelry clippers to snip the heads off the head pins.

About two-thirds in from the outside edge, push a pin into the top of one boot. Do the same with the other boot.

With the boots standing on a firm, flat surface, center the body on the protruding pins and push down to meet the boots. Raise the body slightly and use the tip of a bamboo skewer to dab a bit of E6000 glue on top of each boot around the head pin, then push down and allow to dry.

Push the remaining pin halfway into the bottom of the head. Center the head on top of the body, work the head pin through the felting, and move it down into the body until the two pieces meet. Don't glue between the pieces, so you can turn the head whichever way you like.

Felt the nose and eyes onto the face using red and black wool. This time you want to pack the felt and build it up slightly to make gumdrop-like, three-dimensional features. To make the snowman's mouth you can use wool roving to felt a thin smile, or you can dab the center inch of a 2-inch (5-cm) piece of black embroidery thread with E6000 glue, position it on the face to make a smile, let dry, then snip off the ends.

Assembling the body and giving your snowman a face will help you envision and place the arms.

To make the arms, pull off two pieces of white wool roving, each about 3½ inches square (9 cm square). Roll one piece into a cylinder and lay it on the foam mat or stacked sponges. The purpose of the mat is to keep the needle from breaking. You don't want to pierce the mat itself, or you might end up with an arm felted to it! The object here is to use the felting needle to shape the arm and build it up, adding more felt as needed to make it about ½ inch (12 mm) thick. Because you are shaping and compressing the wool, place your jabs close together. Leave the top ½ inch (12 mm) of the wool at the top of each arm unfelted—this is where you will felt it seamlessly to the body. Shape the arm that will hold the tree in a slightly crooked position and the other arm in a looser curve. Shape the hands like mittens, thumbs to the inside.

To get the right placement for the arms, use straight pins to hold them lightly in place.

To attach the arms, felt the loose wool at the top of the arm to the body. Lay a bit more wool over the arm and felt to the body, molding it over the arm and jabbing more frequently to make a clear indentation where it joins the body. Only the loose wool at the top and the upper part of the other arm need to be felted to the body.

Wrap the chenille craft stem around the snowman's neck and twist the ends to look like a scarf caught in the wind.

If your tree has a base on it, use jewelry clippers to remove the base, leaving a little less than ½ inch (12 mm) of tree trunk. Position the tree in the crook of the snowman's arm, using the bit of wire trunk as a prong to help lodge it firmly.

Let it snow!

LUCKY PINECONES

How did pinecones become one of the first and most enduring decorations for Christmas trees, Christmas centerpieces, and wreaths? The obvious answer is that early decorations were made almost wholly of natural items—nuts, fruits, and berries. While this is true, the actual story dates back to a Christmas legend that exists, in different versions, throughout Scandinavia and Germany.

THE SILVER PINECONE

Once upon a time, as Christmas approached, a woodcutter and his family found themselves without any money to buy presents for their neighbors. They did not mind doing without gifts themselves, but to be unable to give anything to friends hurt them grievously. Living with the family was a little wooden elf who watched over the household from his perch on the mantle. After the family had gone to bed, he climbed down from his perch and left a note telling them how to solve their problem. He advised them to gather all the pinecones they could find, for not only did pinecones make good decorations, they could also be used as fuel to keep their friends warm.

The woodcutter, his wife, and their little children spent all the next day doing just that. They came home from their day in the woods with a bag of pinecones for each of their friends, too tired to even eat their bread and soup for dinner. When they woke the next morning, they prepared to distribute their pinecones, for it was now Christmas Eve. To their amazement, each pinecone had turned to pure silver. For a moment, the parents thought of all the food those pinecones could buy, and the children thought of toys and sweets. In the end, though, they decided it would be wrong to keep them and gave them to their friends as planned.

That night, Nisse, the Christmas gnome, arrived at the cottage just as the family returned. The children were beside themselves with excitement, for Nisse only

showed himself to children who had been very, very good. He left the family a majestic pinecone, which they placed on the mantel beside the little elf. When the family woke in the morning, they saw the pinecone gleaming bright silver, for it too had turned into precious metal. From that day on, good luck followed each member of the family, and they were never in want again.

MATERIALS

Kosher salt

Resealable plastic bags

Food coloring, paste or liquid

Mod Podge

Paintbrush

Pinecones

A shallow bowl for each color

HOW-TO

You can make your cones any color you want. We mixed a few different blues and greens for ours. To mix colors, place a fair amount of salt in a resealable plastic bag and add a drop or two of food coloring. You can use the coloring as is or mix to get different variations, such as using blue and green to make aqua, and so on. Add the food coloring sparingly, especially if you're using the paste type. The colors are concentrated, and you can always add more if the shade is too pale.

Seal the bag and knead with your fingers to work the coloring into the salt.

Apply Mod Podge to the pinecone by liberally painting the top side and edges of the leaves.

Pour the colored salt over the cone over a bowl to catch the excess salt and turn to coat each side. Set aside to dry. Repeat until you reach your desired consistency.

Tip: Make some cones with untinted salt. They contrast nicely with the colored cones, and when Christmas is over and the decorations are put away, a basket of "snowy" cones transitions to January and keeps the house from feeling suddenly bare.

TABLETOP TREE

People today often lament that "real" trees have been replaced by artificial ones or pint-sized replicas. The truth is, touches of artificiality have always been a part of Christmas decorations. In the nineteenthth and twentieth centuries, both cotton and soap flakes were used as snow to decorate tree branches. During World War II, when hale and hearty young men were off fighting, trees were in short supply because there was no one to do the work of cutting them down and trucking them to the cities. The trees that were available during those years sold for prices never seen before, and many families opted to skip the time-honored symbol until peace returned.

While the World War II shortages of real trees prevailed, tabletop trees came into fashion, along with the small bottlebrush trees that are now associated with that bygone era. For enterprising homemakers, there were patterns for tabletop trees made of all sorts of materials, from felt to painted balsa wood to our favorite, tulle net.

MATERIALS

One 9-inch (23-mm) Styrofoam cone

Acrylic craft paint in the same shade as the tulle net

Paintbrush

25-yard (22.8-m) roll of 6-inch- (15-cm-) wide tulle net
Note: You can also use 3½ yards (3.2 m) of 45-inch- (115-cm-) wide tulle off the bolt, but buying it in roll form will save you lots of cutting and measuring

Embroidery or tapestry needle

Embroidery thread (floss) in the same shade as the tulle net

Straight pins

Glitter, artificial snow, or miniature garland and ornaments, as desired

Paint the Styrofoam cone to match the color of tulle you've chosen. If you are using thick paint from a tube, thin it with a bit of water so it goes on smoothly.

Measure and cut a piece of net long enough to go around the base of the cone twice. Now cut the piece lengthwise down the center, so you have two 3-inch- (7.5-cm-) wide pieces.

Cut a piece of thread long enough to go around the base of the tree about one and a half times and thread the needle with 2 strands of floss.

Fold a piece of net in half lengthwise. Working close to the raw edges, stitch through both layers and pull the thread taut to form a ruffle. When you reach the end of the first piece, fold the remaining piece in half lengthwise and gather it on the same needle and thread.

With the folded side out, attach the raw edges of the ruffle along the stitching line to the cone with straight pins. Halfway around the base, anchor the end of the first piece and the beginning of the second piece, pulling the thread and adjusting the ruffle so that it fits snugly. To complete the row, overlap and anchor the end of the second piece to the form where the first piece begins, pulling the thread and adjusting the ruffle to fit. Knot and cut the thread. Anchor the ruffle at intervals between the first 4 pins. Your first row is done.

Following the same procedure, make a second row ¼ to ½ inch (6 to 12 mm) above the first, depending on how or stiff or thick your tulle is.

Continue adding rows at even intervals, measuring each time to cut a length of net twice the circumference of the row.

About one-third of the way up, begin to stitch about ½ inch (12 mm) from the raw edges. You want to make sure the ruffles mimic the shape of the cone, so you must adjust your stitching line to make sure your tree has a nice taper.

By the time you are about one-quarter of the way from the top, your stitching should be almost in the middle of the folded strip. As you near the very top and the circumference of the cone becomes very small, add a final ruffle in a spiral, rather than making individual pieces for rows. Angle your pins downward so they don't come out the other side of the narrow cone.

Pull the final bit of ruffle up to make a nice tip for your tree.

When you're done, look for bare spots and adjust the ruffles as needed. If there's a spot where your rows got too far apart, you can sneak an extra row in.

You can leave your tree plain, sprinkle a bit of glitter or artificial snow over it, or add miniature garlands and ornaments for decoration.

CHRISTMAS CRACKERS

Christmas Crackers are a British tradition, but their inspiration originated on a trip to Paris. In 1846, British resident Thomas Smith visited the City of Light and saw local vendors selling sugared almonds wrapped in a twist of tissue. He took the idea home to England and did a brisk holiday business selling the wrapped sweets. Noticing that the treats were often bought by men to give to women, he began including a short love poem inside the wrapper. Soon everyone was selling individually wrapped nuts and sweets, so Smith replaced the twist with a tube, added more sweets and, in the 1860s, added the "crackers," chemically treated strips that would make a popping sound when sharply pulled. To stay ahead of the competition, Smith upped the ante by adding a small gift. In the early 1900s, Smith's sons, who inherited the business, added paper hats resembling crowns. In the 1930s, during the Depression, jokes, limericks, and riddles replaced the love poems. Once all but unknown in the United States, the crackers have been steadily growing in popularity since the 1980s. Today, Christmas crackers are commercially available almost everywhere, with prices varying depending on the value of the trinkets inside. But it's more fun to make your own!

MATERIALS

Empty paper towel tubes, 1 for every 2 crackers

Scissors or craft knife

Crepe paper in 3 or 4 different colors

Ruler

Double-sided tape, glue dots, or hot glue gun with hot glue sticks

Snap strips, 1 for each cracker

Embellishments such as Dresden trim, die cuts, stickers, and charms

Ribbons, berries on wired stems, wired tinsel, or chenille craft stems to use as ties

Wrapped candies, nuts, fortunes, riddles, trinkets, and paper crowns (instructions following) to fill each cracker

Cut the paper towel tubes into 2 pieces of equal length.

For each cracker, cut a piece of crepe paper that measures 12 by 14 inches (30.5 by 35.5 cm), with the grain of the paper running parallel to the short side. If you are using something other than a paper towel holder for your tube, cut a piece of crepe paper the length of the tube plus 7 inches (18 cm) and twice the circumference plus 1 inch (2.5 cm).

Fold the crepe paper in half with the right side out by bringing the two short edges together and making a firm crease on the folded edge. You will end up with a double-layered piece of paper that measures 12 by 7 inches (30.5 by 18 cm).

Tape or glue the raw edges of the crepe paper to the tube. Center a snap strip on the outside of the tube across from the taped edge, and hold it in place as you wrap the crepe paper over it and around the tube. Secure the end in place with tape or glue.

Decorate the tube with the elements and embellishments you've chosen, using glue dots or double-sided tape to attach them.

Use ribbon, a wired tie-on, tinsel wire, or a chenille stem to close one end of the tube. Make sure the snap strip extends past the tie-off.

Fill the tube with candies, trinkets, jokes or riddles, and a paper crown (see instructions below), then tie off the open end, again making sure the snap strip extends beyond the tie-off point. If the snap strip extends beyond the crepe paper, trim to make it even.

PAPER CROWN

Paper crowns have been a staple in Christmas crackers since the early 1900s. Traditionally they're made of tissue paper, but crepe paper is more durable and, being stretchy, makes a better fit. Use several different colors for a colorful group at the holiday table.

For each crown, cut a strip of crepe paper that measures 4 by 24 inches (10 by 61 cm). Cut so the grain of the paper runs parallel to the short (4-inch [10-cm]) side.

Overlap the ends and fasten together with double-sided tape to form the crown.

To make the crown points, fold the crown in half, then fold in half three more times, so you have a tidy package 1½ by 4 inches (4 by 10 cm). Cut from the top of the folded side down and across to the other side at a roughly 45-degree angle to make the points of the crown. Your crown is finished and ready to wear.

MAKE THE POP

Crackers are traditionally opened when everyone is gathered at the Christmas table, either before or after the meal is served. To make the cracker pop, grasp firmly at the tie-off at each end and pull quickly and firmly, making sure you are grasping the snap strip as well as the paper. It's perfectly acceptable to pop your own cracker, but it's more fun as a shared event. You and your neighbor at the table can each take an end, but the ultimate is a group pop. To do this, each person at the table crosses one arm over the other, grasps their own cracker with the right hand, the cracker of the neighbor to their right with the left hand. On the count of three, everyone tugs at once, hoping for the loudest crack possible.

PERSONALIZE IT

Making your own crackers offers a chance to personalize the contents. You can choose trinkets appropriate for each guest and replace jokes and riddles with a prediction for the coming year or a wish for a particular stroke of good fortune. You can also make a game by asking each person who will be attending to submit a secret about themselves to you in advance. The secret should be lighthearted, fun, and known to no one else, such as the grandparents who had a Jell-O fight as newlyweds. Put one secret in each cracker, and the person who receives it reads it aloud and tries to guess, along with the other guests, whose secret it is. When you make personalized crackers, add a name tag for each one.

PINECONE WREATH

Wreaths date back to the ancient world, when they were worn as personal adornments on special occasions. Victorious athletes were crowned with laurel wreaths, and brides wore garlands of flowers in their hair. In addition to signifying triumph, wreaths symbolized hope and promise for the future. It was a short leap for early Christians to adapt the custom to signify the coming of Christ. Christmas wreaths were popular in Germany as early as the Renaissance. Unlike people living in warmer climates who had holly and ivy to decorate with, the Germans used the only greenery available in midwinter—pine boughs—to weave into wreaths. Early wreaths were decorated with four violet candles, one for each week of Advent. On Christmas Eve, a pink or rose candle, placed in the center of the wreath, was lit to symbolize the birth of Christ. Though the hazardous candles have disappeared, the custom of decorated wreaths lives on, and the final, rose-colored candle of warmth

MATERIALS

5-by-5-inch (12-by-12-cm) piece of light- or medium-weight cardboard

Pencil

Ruler

Compass

Sharp kitchen shears

4 to 5 dozen 1- to 1½-inch- (2.5- to 4-cm-) long young pinecones

Note: If your pinecones are so dry they shatter when you cut them, soak them in water for a while, and when they're almost completely dry, try again.

E6000 glue

Tweezers

Ribbon or vintage rayon seam binding, ½ inch wide by 2 feet long (12 mm by 61 cm)

and hope can still be seen in red bows and ribbons.

HOW-TO

Draw a circle 3½ to 4 inches (9 to 10 cm) in diameter on the piece of cardboard with a compass. Draw a circle 2 inches (5 cm) in diameter centered inside the first to make a donut shape.

Cut out the ring to create the base of the wreath.

Cut the top off one of the pinecones about ½ inch (12 mm) down with kitchen shears. You'll see that the top resembles a tiny rose, or the type of succulent plant known as hen and chicks. This is the part you're going to use. Reserve the bottoms.

Cut the tops off the remaining pinecones and begin gluing them to the cardboard foundation. While you can use any craft glue, E6000 glue is preferred because it dries quickly and is less runny than most craft glues.

Continue gluing tops to cover the whole wreath. Let them slant in different directions and extend over the edges to create a natural placement. Cut bits and petals from the bottoms of the cones to fill in bare spots, using tweezers to wedge the pieces into place.

Allow the wreath to dry, then cut the ribbon in half and glue the fold to the back side of the cardboard at the center top.

When the ribbon is dry, tie into a bow and hang on a flat surface. To use as a tree ornament, cut more pinecone roses and finish the back side as you did the front.

SPARKLING SNOWFLAKES

Although Descartes wrote a description of snowflakes as early as the 1630s, they didn't become an object of widespread interest until the invention of the microscope a few decades later. Scientists were fascinated by their six-sided symmetry, and the realization that snowflakes were as individual as people resulted in elaborate prints and drawings that captured the popular imagination. Over the centuries, snowflakes became a popular motif for painters, knitters of mittens and sweaters, and, of course, schoolchildren with scissors and paper.

MATERIALS

Wax paper

Rolling pin

4-ounce (115-g) pouch of Crayola Model Magic ready-mixed, air-dry clay in white or bisque

R&M 5-Piece Snowflake Cookie Cutter Set, or snowflake cookie cutters and small aspic cutters

Bamboo skewer

Metal spatula

Mod Podge

Paintbrush

Glitter in assorted colors

Saucer or flat bowl for every color of glitter you use

Ribbon, string, or clear nylon thread, for hanging

HOW-TO

Spread a sheet of wax paper on the counter.

With the rolling pin, roll some of the clay out to a thickness of about ¼ inch (6 mm) and cut snowflakes with the cookie cutters. Pull away the excess clay and return to the pouch.

Use the small cutters that came with the set or other small aspic cutters to cut designs into the snowflakes.

If necessary, use the pointed end of a bamboo skewer to remove any bits of clay that did not come away with the small cutters.

Use the blunt end of the skewer to make a hole for the hanger.

Transfer the snowflakes with a metal spatula to a clean, flat surface to dry for 24 to 48 hours, turning once every 12 hours to prevent bowing. They will remain slightly spongy but will be firm and hold their shape.

When the snowflakes are dry, paint one side with Mod Podge. Make sure to paint the edges of the snowflake and inside the cutouts as well.

Lay the snowflake, glue side up, in a saucer and pour glitter liberally over it, enough to bury the flake.

Wait a few minutes, then gently lift the snowflake. Reapply glitter to any bare spots. It's okay to add more glue—since Mod Podge dries clear, you won't see where it was reapplied.

Repeat with the remaining snowflakes. Set the flakes aside and allow to dry overnight.

The next day, apply glue and glitter the reverse side and let dry.

When snowflakes are fully dry, thread with ribbon, string, or clear nylon thread and knot to form a hanger.

LITTLE SNOWMAN

So little is known about the origins of snowmen that when humorist Bob Eckstein wrote a purported history a few years ago, many embraced the book as fact. Since the first verified use of the word "snowman" didn't occur until 1829, it seems the snowman is a relatively modern invention, possibly North American. Although Scandinavians had access to plenty of snow, their preferred yuletide figures are huge goats made of straw. Regardless of its origins, nowhere is the snowman as popular as in the United States, where Gene Autry's 1950 recording of "Frosty the Snowman," along with subsequent book, television show, and movie spin-offs, have made him an enduring symbol of the season.

MATERIALS

One 1½-inch (4-cm) Styrofoam ball

Two 1-inch (2.5-cm) Styrofoam balls

Mod Podge or white craft glue

Paintbrush

Paring knife

Artificial snow, such as vintage-style mica flakes, Epsom salt, or large-crystal salt (see Sources, page 144)

White paint (if using Epsom salt or large-crystal salt)

E6000 glue

Black glitter or embossing powder

Safety glasses

Jewelry clippers or kitchen shears

3 head pins, ½ inch (12 mm) long (straight pins can be substituted)

Toothpicks

3 straight pins

1 red seed bead, for nose

2 opaque black seed beads, for eyes

1 inch (2.5 cm) of black embroidery thread (all 6 strands)

2 small twigs, real or artificial, or 2 artificial pine needles, for arms

Four 9-mm jingle bells or small snowflake charms

6 inches (15 cm) of red embroidery thread (all 6 strands)

Paint the 1½-inch (4-cm) Styrofoam ball and one of the 1-inch (2.5-cm) Styrofoam balls with Mod Podge (or white craft glue diluted with a bit of water) and roll in artificial snowflakes, Epsom salt, or large-crystal salt. Set aside to dry.

Cut the remaining 1-inch (2.5-cm) ball in half with a paring knife. With the cut side down, trim about ¼ inch (6 mm) off one side of each ball. Glue the freshly cut sides together with E6000 glue to form the boots.

When the glue on the boots is dry, paint the piece with Mod Podge and cover with black glitter or embossing powder.

Wearing safety glasses, clip the heads off the head pins (or straight pins) with the jewelry cutters. Push one head pin into each boot about ¼ inch (6 mm) from the center join.

Center the 1½-inch (4-cm) ball onto the protruding head pins and push down to meet the boots.

Center the remaining head pin and push halfway into the body. Attach the head.

Check to make sure your snowman's parts are centered and balanced. Correct if needed. Use the tip of a toothpick to dab glue between the parts.

Wearing safety glasses, snip off the sharp end of three straight pins. Thread a red bead on one and push into the front center of the head for the nose. Thread each remaining pin with a black bead and add them as eyes.

Use a toothpick to dab the middle ½ inch (12 mm) of the black embroidery thread with E6000 glue. Position it on the face to make a smile. Let dry, then snip off the ends.

Add twigs or artificial pine needles as arms.

Knot the jingle bells to the red embroidery thread at ¾-inch (2-cm) intervals. Use a dab of E6000 glue to attach the ends to the twig arms.

SANTA STAR ORNAMENT

In the late nineteenth and early twentieth centuries, glass ornaments were a leading cottage industry in Germany, where whole families would work at painting balls, figures, and other fanciful shapes for export to America and other countries. The handiwork made the ornaments quite expensive, and the idea of buying several at once would have sent most people into a swoon. Each ornament was sold individually, and even comfortably well-off families formed the habit of adding just one or two ornaments to their collection each year. It could take a lifetime to accumulate enough of them to decorate the ornament-laden trees we're used to today. During this time, electric lights were also a rarity. Even if the house had electricity, the cost of purchasing a single string of a dozen lights could be the equivalent of $40 or $50 in today's currency. And since the string used regular-size, full-wattage bulbs, the bill from the electric company could be quite high.

Yet, despite the lack of balls and lights, trees looked lavish. Tinsel and garlands glittered, and in place of glass ornaments there were die-cut pictures. The pictures were beautifully detailed and printed in vivid, sumptuous color on creamy, heavy-weight paper. In an era when color had yet to enliven magazine pages, this was a treat in itself. The images were often embossed with gold, silver, and tracings of glitter. Less costly than the hand-painted imported glass balls and stars, the die-cuts were the dominant decoration of their time.

Though made specifically to adorn Christmas trees, scenes depicted on the die-cuts were not necessarily geared to the holiday or even to winter. Roses, horseshoes adorned with shamrocks, delicate hands holding violets, and patriotic themes were all common. Our Santa star ornament pays homage to their heyday.

MATERIALS

2 pieces of lightweight cardboard, such as from a cereal box, each larger than the star you want to make

Pencil

Scissors

E6000 glue

Mod Podge

Paintbrush

Shallow, flat-bottomed pan, such as a round cake pan

Glitter

12-inch (30.5-cm) length of embroidery thread (all 6 strands)

Ruler

Small Christmas charm

HOW-TO

Trace or photocopy and cut out the image on page 50 at 150% to make a star template. The star should measure 7 inches (18 cm) at its widest point. Cut out and tape the template to the unprinted side of one of the pieces of cardboard and cut out the inner and outer star lines.

Use the star you just made to trace and cut another star from the remaining piece of cardboard.

With the plain, unprinted cardboard facing out, glue the two stars together. Leave one of the star tips open and unglued.

When dry, paint one side of the star with Mod Podge. Place the star, glue side up, in the flat pan and liberally pour on the glitter so the star is completely buried. Wait a few minutes, then retrieve the star and shake off the excess glitter. Let dry completely and repeat the process, painting Mod Podge directly over the first layer. When the second layer of glitter is completely dry, repeat the process on the other side. Make sure to get the edges of both the outer star and inner star shape.

When the star is completely dry, cut an 8-inch (20-cm) piece of embroidery thread. Use E6000 to glue the ends of the thread between the pieces of the star tip you left open. Add more glue inside to glue the tip of the star together. Set a book on top until dry.

Feed the remaining embroidery thread trough the loop of the charm. Knot the ends together. Check for positioning, then use E6000 glue to attach the knot to the back of the star so the charm hangs in the center. Allow to dry for a few minutes before hanging.

TRINKET BOX

One of the most enduring and overlooked legacies of the Victorian era is a fondness for packaging. Like us, the Victorians liked to make things pretty, bright, and interesting. They knew that even a small item seemed more important if its packaging created a stir of excitement, and greeting cards and gift wrap both came about during this era. A perfect example of this took place during the 1902 Christmas season. Although animal crackers had been around since the 1880s, the product took off when the cookies were packaged in a circus-themed box fitted with a string so it could be hung from the tree branches. This was an instant hit, and the package is with us still.

This was also a time when women made their first steps into the paid labor market, and many families left the farm for the city. Because of this, consumer goods continued to proliferate and gift-giving was no longer confined to family members. Advice columns of the era are full of questions about what to give and how much one needed to spend, as well as complaints about the growing list of people who needed gifts or at least to be added to the ever-lengthening greeting card list. Whether giving someone homemade candy or gold cufflinks, there was one thing on which all the experts agreed: Put it in a pretty box.

MATERIALS

Round papier mâché box, 4 by 2 inches (10 by 5 cm)

Tape measure

Acrylic craft paint, your choice of colors

Paintbrush

Mod Podge

2 clean, shallow bowls

Glitter that harmonizes with the decorative paper

12½-by-2½-inch (32-by-6-cm) piece of Scotch Positionable Mounting Adhesive, or similar mounting adhesive

Bone folder (optional)

12-by-2-inch (30.5-by-5-cm) piece of decorative paper, such as scrapbooking paper

Before you cut your decorative paper, measure the exact circumference of your box base. Technically, the circumference of a round 4-inch (10-cm) diameter box would be 12.56 inches (31.9 cm), but because the box is slightly smaller than the lid, we found that the length of a 12-inch (30.5-cm) square of scrapbook paper worked just fine on the boxes we tried.

Paint the inside of the box and the inside of the box lid with acrylic craft paint. When dry, paint a thin coat of Mod Podge over it and allow to dry.

Paint the top and sides of the lid with Mod Podge. Holding the wet lid over one of the bowls, pour on the glitter in abundance. Roll the sides of the lid in the glitter that's fallen in the bowl. Allow to set a few minutes, then tap off the excess and set aside to dry. Don't worry if there are thin or bare spots—you're going to apply a second coat later.

Apply the positionable mounting adhesive to the outside of the box. Use a bone folder or your fingers to go over the adhesive several times, pressing firmly to make a strong bond.

Trim off excess, peel off the covering, and apply the decorative paper to the sticky sides of the box, pressing and smoothing all the way around to attach firmly.

When the glittered lid is dry, paint a layer of Mod Podge directly over the glitter. Holding the lid over the second bowl, pour the glitter from the first bowl over it and repeat the glittering process. Excess glitter can be brushed back into the container and reused.

FLOURISH

If you want to add a whimsical touch to your creation, cut out a small seasonal motif such as bells or a Santa from your favorite piece of wrapping or other decorative paper and use Mod Podge to affix it to the inside bottom of the box. When it's dry, seal in place with a second coat of Mod Podge.

CANDY STRIPE
CHRISTMAS STOCKING

When newspaperman Francis Church answered an eight-year-old reader's question about the existence of Santa Claus with the famous, "Yes, Virginia, there is a Santa Claus," he wasn't just comforting a young girl—he was actually telling the truth. Saint Nicholas, from whom Santa Claus derives, was a fourth-century bishop in what is now Turkey. Born into wealth, he used his inheritance to help the poor. Legend has it that a story reached him of a village family who was so poor there was no dowry for the three daughters, and the parents despaired over the fate of the girls. In the dark of night, Nicholas made his way to the family's house and tossed golden coins through an open window. Before retiring for the night, the daughters had washed out their stockings and hung them near the hearth to dry. Some of the coins caught in the folds of the stockings, while others landed on the floor nearby. In the morning, the family rejoiced to find the miraculous gift—enough coins to provide each girl with a dowry.

Nicholas performed similar good deeds throughout his life. When he was elevated to sainthood, St. Nicholas Day fell in December. The tradition of giving to the poor at yuletide became a tradition, and the children's version became a Christmas stocking filled with treats. Even in hard times, an anonymous stranger providing for the poor became a way of delighting and treating children on Christmas morning, and St. Nicholas became Santa Claus. But the most unchanged part of the original legend may be the stocking itself, a reminder of the three daughters and the joy people find in giving to others.

One 11-by-17 inch (28-by-43-cm) sheet of paper to make a pattern

Pencil

Ruler, preferably a clear, 2-inch (5-cm) wide quilter's ruler

Scissors

Straight pins

Two 12-by-20-inch (30.5-by-50-cm) pieces white felt

5 yards (4.6 m) 6-mm red string sequins

4 yards (3.7 m) Terrifically Tacky Tape

Red embroidery thread (all 6 strands)

Straight pins

Big-eye needle, such as for needlepoint or counted cross-stitch

E6000 glue

HOW-TO

On the sheet of paper, draw a pattern for the stocking. It should take up most of the paper, with a foot that measures about 11 inches (28 cm) from heel to toe.

Cut out the pattern. Pin the pattern to the felt and cut out each piece of felt separately. Save the felt scraps.

On the piece of felt that will be the front of the stocking, use the pencil to draw diagonal lines at 1½-inch (4-cm) intervals. Don't worry about the pencil lines; they'll be covered by the sequins.

Use a pin to unthread several sequins, making enough free string to tie a knot close to the first sequin on the line. Snip off the end and set the sequins aside.

Run a strip of tape along one of the pencil lines. (It doesn't matter which order you do the lines in.) Leave the tape's liner on.

Peel back a few inches of the liner. Place the first sequin at the edge of the stocking and press firmly to attach. Continue peeling back a few inches of the liner at a time and pressing with your fingertips to make a firm bond. When you near the end, cut the sequin string about 1 inch (2.5 cm) longer then needed. Figure out which sequin will be the last one at the edge of the stocking. Unthread the sequins that come after it and tie a knot underneath the final sequin. Snip the ends and press firmly onto the tape.

Repeat to create the remaining stripes and a border at the top edge of the stocking.

Pin the front stocking to the back stocking, right sides facing out. Using all 6 strands of the embroidery thread in the big-eye needle, sew the pieces together by making French knots all the way around the edges, making about three French knots per inch. Leave the top edge of the stocking open.

Cut a 5-by-1-inch (12-by-2.5-cm) strip from the scraps. Following the directions above, make a stripe of sequins down the center of the strip. Fold the strip in half and glue the ends together with E6000 glue. Give it a few minutes to set, then glue the ends to the inside of the stocking at the back of the leg to create a loop for hanging. Let dry thoroughly before hanging.

VARIATION

If you're making more than one stocking, try varying the color of felt and sequins, such as using white sequins on red felt, red sequins on green felt, or green sequins on white felt. Striped stockings hanging in a row brighten any mantel.

TIP

When it's time to take down the decorations, roll the stocking around a paper towel tube before you store it to keep it free of creases.

CHRISTMAS BELLS

Bells predate Christmas by many centuries. Originally they were part of many pagan festivals, including Rome's Saturnalia, a winter holiday marked by gift-giving, revelry, and masters waiting on servants at a banquet. Christianity began adopting the use of bells at the beginning of the fifth century, and by early in the medieval era they were common in European churches. During World War II, Britain's church bells fell silent, held in reserve to use as a signal if the country was being invaded.

Even with the proliferation of large and impressive church bells, smaller bells remained popular. In an era before recorded music, when few could afford a musical instrument, bells served to accompany singing and dancing. Bells were the people's instrument, affordable to almost all or made at home from scrap metal. When early carolers made their rounds at yuletide, they customarily had handbells with them. Sometimes they didn't sing at all, but let their bells speak for them. When the first tuned handbells appeared in the early 1700s, bell choirs became a feature of church music, especially during the Christmas season. Over the years, they have become as emblematic of the holiday as candy canes and wreaths.

MATERIALS

One 4-inch (10-cm) and one 2½-inch (6-cm) Styrofoam bell

Mod Podge

Paintbrush

2 clean, shallow bowls for each color of glitter

Glitter, your choice of colors

Dresden trim that will accommodate the curve of the bell

Straight pins

Toothpicks

E6000 glue

Ornament hangers or 2-inch (5-cm) jewelry head pins with an eye loop on one end, one for each bell

Thin silver or gold cord to make a hanger

The easiest way to apply glitter to the bell is in three stages: first the top, then the bottom, and finally the underside. Grasping a bell at the bottom, paint the upper half of the bell with Mod Podge. Holding the bell over a shallow bowl, pour on your choice of glitter, then place the bell in the bowl and roll it in the glitter. Pour on more glitter as needed. Allow to set a few minutes, then tap off the excess. Allow to dry thoroughly.

Holding the bell by the dry upper end, paint the bottom half of the bell with Mod Podge and cover with glitter as described above. Don't be afraid of overlapping; Mod Podge dries clear.

You can glitter the underside of the bell with the same shade of glitter or add dimension by using a second shade. Return unused glitter to the container for future use.

When the bell is dry, place the Dresden trim. The curve of the bell will make it want to spring away, so you may have to change the position slightly or manipulate the motif to find the right spot. Hold it loosely in place with one or two straight pins.

Using a toothpick dipped in E6000, dab glue on the back at several points on half of the motif. Press down with your fingertips until the glue sets enough to hold in place. Allow to dry a few minutes more, then glue the other half to the bell.

Push an ornament hanger or eye-loop head pin into the top of each bell. Thread a length of cord through to make a loop for hanging.

OTHER IDEAS

These bells are pretty on a tree, but they can also be made into a garland to hang from the mantel attached to a swag of pine or a length of tinsel rope. A cluster of different-size bells cascading against a clutch of pine boughs with a bow at the top makes a welcoming and very vintage-looking decoration for the front door.

NOEL BLOCKS

At one time, children's toys and other items played a large role in decorating the house for Christmas, especially among the middle and upper classes. Baby shoes were often hung on the tree, as were silver baby cups and spoons. Toys that were usually confined to the nursery or children's rooms were suddenly unleashed to parade across the parlor floor. Pictures of early-twentieth-century trees show miniature villages rather than gifts beneath the branches. The tree was surrounded by a tiered base covered with snowy drifts of tablecloth on which miniature cattle grazed, horses galloped, and little dogs guarded tiny farmsteads. Noah's ark, a popular toy of the era, revealed carved wooden animals in perfectly matched pairs. Often, one can see an elaborate dollhouse flanking the tree. Toy soldiers, wooden airplanes, dolls—whatever each child loved most seemed to be allowed in the otherwise carefully decorated room.

Wooden blocks have long been a staple children's toy, and they live on in décor and ornaments today.

MATERIALS

4 plain wooden blocks,
1½ inch (4 cm) square

Mod Podge

Paintbrush

2 clean, shallow bowls

Gold glitter

Scissors

E6000 glue

Tiny angel, snowman, deer,
or other figure from a package
tie-on (optional)

To begin, paint a ¼-inch- (6-mm-) wide Mod Podge border all the way around the face of one side of the block, leaving the center bare. Holding the block over one bowl, pour on the glitter. Let set a minute or so, then tap off the excess glitter and set aside to dry. Repeat with one side of each of the remaining blocks, pouring the glitter from one bowl while holding the block over the second bowl.

Do the opposite side of each block in the same way. When the two sides are dry, add glitter to the remaining two sides of each block.

When the four sides are completely dry, paint the entire bottom of a block with Mod Podge and pour on the glitter. Don't worry about getting a bit of glue on the sides that you have already covered with glitter. Tap off the excess glitter and allow to dry with bottoms facing up. Repeat with the remaining blocks.

When the bottoms are completely dry, finish the top of each block in the same way. After the blocks are thoroughly dry, touch up any spots that need it.

Copy or scan and print the NOEL squares on page 141. Cut out each letter along the lines. Use Mod Podge to attach an N to each side of one block, an O to each side of another block, and Es and Ls to the remaining two blocks.

Use a dab of E6000 to attach a small angel, snowman, or other figure to the top of one of the blocks if you desire.

VARIATION

Blocks left over? Transform them into tree ornaments. Apply glitter to each side or paint with acrylic craft paint and attach cutouts of Christmas and winter motifs such as snowflakes, mittens, sleds, gingerbread men, and stockings. Center a small eye screw at the top, then thread with narrow ribbon or cord to make a loop for hanging.

SANTA NAPKINS

The tradition of handmade gifts is a long one, especially for women. While men usually gave possessions, up until the Industrial Revolution, women seldom had possessions to give. What they gave was likely to be handmade and signified a personal connection to the recipient. When *Gone with the Wind*'s Melanie made Ashley a Confederate jacket for Christmas, she was giving a gift only a wife or mother might. But Scarlett staked her own claim by cutting up one of her shawls to make a matching sash for him, a gift that implied a high degree of personal connection with romantic overtones. This excerpt from *Harper's Bazaar* adds insight into the personal nature of Victorian gift-making:

A Lady cannot give a gentleman a gift of great value because he would certainly feel bound to return one still more valuable and thus her gift would lose all its grace and retain only a selfish commercial aspect. What, then, shall she give? Here is the woman's advantage. She has her hands, while men must transact all their present-giving in hard cash. She can hem fine handkerchiefs—and in order to give them intrinsic value, if their relationship warrants such a favor, she can embroider the name or monogram with her own hair.

—Harper's Bazaar, *1879*

Magazines of the day published lists of gift-giving ideas and supplied the patterns for making them. Work began months ahead of the holiday, and far from feeling pressured by the extra work, women looked forward to spending time together as they worked on their gifts. For a time, it seemed like the plush period of the 1920s, the proliferation of manufactured goods, and the faster pace of life would put an end to the tradition of holiday needlework. Hard times brought the tradition back, and during the Depression, tea towels and dresser scarves embroidered with patterns printed in the Sunday paper were favorite gift items among friends, while close family members received grander projects like quilts and tablecoths. Our Santa napkins are a tribute to a style of embroidery known as Redwork, a design worked entirely in red, which became popular in the late 1800s when Turkish cotton manufacturers perfected the first colorfast red dye.

MATERIALS

Tracing paper

Pen or pencil

Iron

20-inch (50-cm) plain white cloth napkins

Light box (optional)

Painter's tape or masking tape (optional)

Fine-point light-tan Sharpie or transfer pen or pencil

8-inch (20-cm) embroidery hoop

Embroidery needle

Red DMC embroidery thread

HOW-TO

Position the tracing paper over the images on pages 142–143 and copy onto the tracing paper with the pen. Iron your napkins, if needed.

There are two ways to transfer the designs onto the cloth. If you have a light box, attach the design to the surface with painter's tape or masking tape. Position the napkin over the design and trace lightly with the Sharpie. Your stitches will cover the lines you make. The second method is to flip the tracing paper over, trace the design with a transfer pen or pencil, and iron it onto the napkin.

Place a napkin in the embroidery hoop. Thread your embroidery needle with 3 strands of the red thread and work the design using a backstitch. To make a backstitch, make a single straight stitch as long as you'd like. Bring the needle up through the underside of the fabric a space ahead and back down into the last stitch you made.

DIORAMA ORNAMENT

Until World War II, Germany supplied most of the world's handcrafted Christmas ornaments. After the war, a new player dominated the field: Japan. Occupied by the United States from the surrender to 1952, Japan got American help in recovering from the devastation, but it's doubtful anyone foresaw the country's overnight leap from ruins to an industrial powerhouse. Goods appealing to Western tastes flooded the market, and the workmanship was of higher quality than prewar exports. To overcome the stigma of buying from our recent enemies, the "Made in Japan" stamp was replaced with "Made in Occupied Japan." And the Japanese, eager to modernize and compete, were quick to understand the American obsession with novelty. Among the ornaments they made in mass numbers were dioramas—indented balls with miniature scenes inside.

MATERIALS

2½-inch (6-cm) papier mâché round ball ornament, with hanger

Ruler

Pencil

Very strong kitchen shears or clippers

Tin can (optional)

Aleene's Glitter Snow

Paintbrush

Piece of white cardstock or index card

Compass

Acrylic craft paints

Mod Podge

Twinklets Diamond Dust

7-inch (18-cm) length of light-blue ⅛-inch- (3-mm-) wide ribbon (optional)

Toothpick or needle

1½-inch-(4-cm-) tall bottlebrush tree

E6000 glue

Miniature deer

Small, clean saucer

On the surface of the ornament, make a dot with a pencil midway between the north and south poles. Measure 1 inch (2.5 cm) out from the dot and make a mark where 12:00 would be. Make a second mark at 1:00. Repeat all the way around, then connect the dots to make a circle.

Now comes the hardest part of the project. The papier mâché ornament is comprised of surface wrapping over an extremely tough plastic ball. Make a slit anywhere you can on the inside of the circle with kitchen shears. The easiest way is to prop the ball in a tin can of similar circumference and use the point of the scissors to work an opening. When the opening is big enough, start cutting. Go all the away around the circle you drew. You needn't worry about making the edge smooth and neat.

Pull the hanger loop out through the inside and set aside.

Paint the inside of the ball with glitter snow. If needed, apply a second coat.

On the white cardstock or index card, draw a circle 2 inches (5 cm) in diameter. If you don't have a compass or anything to trace around, you can use the same method you used to draw the circle on the ball. Draw a small tab on the left and right sides at the circle's widest point.

Cut out the circle and fold the tabs under. This will be the platform for your tableau. Insert the circle to check the fit. It should settle even with or slightly below the bottom edge of the hole you cut in the ball. You may need to trim and adjust a bit, but the platform does not need to be perfect, just smooth and level.

When the platform is dry, fit it into the ball. Make sure it's not slanting to one side or the other, then secure it in place by painting glitter snow around the edge to make a seam. Allow to dry.

Paint the outside of the ball with acrylic paint.

When the ball is completely dry, paint the outside with Mod Podge and sprinkle liberally with Diamond Dust.

Knot the ribbon (if using) and trim the end, then use a toothpick or the blunt end of a needle to push the ribbon up through the hole in the top of the ball, or replace the hanger loop.

Glue the tree in place on the platform with E6000 glue. Paint the base of the tree and most of the platform with glitter snow, leaving a spot for the deer bare. When the snow is dry, glue the deer in place.

Pour a generous amount of Diamond Dust into the saucer. Use a toothpick to spread a thin line of E6000 glue around the raw edge of the ball, then press down into the Diamond Dust. Let dry and repeat.

HOLIDAY CHARM BRACELET

"Fashion trendsetter" isn't exactly the tag we think of when it comes to Queen Victoria, but so she was. From her ascension to the throne in 1837 until her death in 1901, she shaped the beliefs, mores, furniture, and fashions of much of the English speaking world. Her taste in clothing gave us trends that have since become givens, including the preference for white wedding dresses and the custom of wearing black to funerals. Though charms and amulets had been worn since ancient times to ward off spirits and bring luck, it was the young Victoria who introduced the modern charm bracelet, an adornment with personal attachment, meant to grow more meaningful and decorative over time. In addition to wearing bracelets of her own, Victoria often gave charms as gifts. Thus, charm bracelets became associated with the queen's favor, and their popularity soared. In America, Tiffany's introduced their first charm bracelet—the classic chain with a single heart—in 1889.

During Victoria's reign, jewelry became not just an adornment but an expression of personal feeling and sentiment. There was jewelry for every mood and occasion and, taking their cue from the queen, women wore not just one or two pieces at a time but several: Earrings, a cameo at the throat, a necklace, and bracelets all worn together were not unusual. Whatever designers could come up with, people were eager to buy, including jewelry that matched the season. This era also saw the first wearing of decorative Christmas pieces, with brooches and pins sporting everything from heralding angels to silver bells and depictions of St. Nicholas. Our charm bracelet pays homage to both.

Clear glass and crystal beads in red and green, assorted shapes and sizes

Head pins in metal tone similar to bracelet chain, 22 gauge, 1½ to 2 inches (4 to 5 cm) long

Safety glasses

Jewelry cutters

Chain-nose jewelry pliers

Jump rings in metal tone similar to bracelet chain

Round-nose jewelry pliers

Red and green plastic holly leaf charms, approximately 18 mm long

Red and green jingle bells, 8-mm size

5 to 7 focal charms with Christmas themes (We used stockings, Santa head, mitten and peppermint candy charms

from Etsy.)

Silver snowflake charms

2 photo frame disks, 18 to 19 mm in diameter, with single loop, in metal tone similar to bracelet chain

E6000 glue

1 clear green flower cap bead, 18-mm size

1 or 2 foil beads in red or green, with gold or silver foil

1 small silver holly charm

Red and green glass bell beads, approximately 8 mm long

1 holly leaf charm with small berries

1 plain chain bracelet that fits loosely around the wrist, with links large enough to accommodate jump rings

HOW-TO

Basics on Bead Loops and Jump Rings

Thread a bead onto a head pin and, wearing safety glasses, trim end of head pin ½ inch (12 mm) from the bead with flush cutters. Bend the pin at a right angle near the base of the bead with chain-nose jewelry pliers and roll toward the bead, making a loop. Pinch the loop firmly at the base to close. To use jump rings, hold the ring with the chain-nose jewelry pliers in one hand use the round-nose jewelry pliers in your other hand to open and close the ring. Give the ring a final, firm pinch when finished to make sure it's completely closed, then clip off any excess head pin with jewelry cutters.

BEAD COMBINATIONS

Gather your beads, findings, and tools and set aside the bead combinations for your bracelet. If you've made jewelry before, you know there's a free-form element involved, so if your beads and combination creations differ from ours, well, that's what makes handcrafted jewelry special. The list of our combinations need not be followed exactly—try varying them for your own unique combinations.

Holly leaf and jingle bell charm: Thread a jump ring through a green plastic holly leaf, thread onto a bell jump ring, and close. Thread an 8-mm green jingle bell onto a jump ring and close.

Stocking charm: Before closing the head pin loop, thread a stocking and a green holly leaf onto the head pin.

Santa head charm: Thread a small red bead or crystal onto a head pin, add Santa head, and form a closed loop.

Mitten charm: Thread a 5-mm green bell bead onto the head pin, top with a red glass bell bead, and close the loop. Thread the mitten with another head pin, form a loop, and thread the bell onto the mitten loop before closing.

Snowflake photo frame charm: Use E6000 glue to attach a snowflake charm to each side of a photo frame disk.

Beaded photo frame charm: We were lucky enough to find small (5-mm) beads that looked like shiny green Christmas balls and fit our photo frame exactly when we placed one in the center surrounded by six more. The easiest way to glue them on is to spread a thin layer of E6000 glue on the photo frame, then quickly arrange and adjust the beads before the glue catches.

Green flower charm: Use E6000 glue to attach a green flower cap bead to a snowflake charm. Let set, then glue a 6-mm red crystal rondelle to the center of the flower.

Red and green bead charm: Thread a 5-mm green bead onto a head pin and top with a 12-mm round red foil bead.

Holly leaf with large berry and silver charm: Fit a green plastic holly leaf with a jump ring and close. Thread a 10-mm red rondelle crystal onto a head pin and make a closed loop. Thread the holly leaf, the crystal, and a silver holly charm onto a jump ring and close the ring.

Red and green mushroom charm: Thread a 10-mm green teardrop onto a head pin, top with a 10-mm red rondelle crystal, and make a closed loop.

Bell beads: Thread a 5-mm green round bead on a head pin, top with a red glass bell bead, and close the loop. Thread a 6-mm red rondelle crystal bead onto a head pin, top with a green glass bell bead, and close the loop.

Gold foil bead dangle: Thread a 6-mm red rondelle crystal bead onto a head pin, top with a red glass bell bead, and close the loop. Thread a 5-mm green round bead on a head pin, top with a gold foil bead, form a loop, and close. Thread both bead combinations onto a jump ring, and close.

Green pineapple charm: Thread a 10-mm green teardrop bead onto a head pin, top with a 6-mm red rondelle crystal, add a green flower cap bead and a small green bead or crystal, then make a closed loop.

BRACELET ASSEMBLY

It's helpful to do a rough layout of your bracelet before you start attaching elements. Lay the chain, unclasped, out straight. Space your focal charms first, keeping your favorites near the middle. Distribute the combinations next, paying attention to color and element, so you don't have too many of the same type or color in one place. Things get disarranged as you work, so you may find it helpful to take a picture of your original layout.

Start attaching elements. Try the bracelet on from time to time to see how it falls and balances out—it's rare to finish a bracelet exactly according to plan, so don't hesitate to move things around. As you work, add more individual beads, bells, and snowflake charms. These not only add to the "loaded" look, but they are also generally shorter than bead combinations and keep your bracelet from looking too neat.

COOKIE PLATE

The idea of setting out cookies for Santa and snacks for his reindeer has its origins in Norse mythology, when the god Odin rode his eight-legged horse through the night sky. Children left straw and sugar in their boots for Odin's horse, and Odin replaced with edible treats and small wooden toys. When the Vikings invaded northern France and their descendants fanned out across Europe, the legends of St. Nicholas merged with Odin and his horse, and the tradition of leaving food out for the mysterious nighttime guest became part of Christmas lore.

MATERIALS

Small plate, such as a dessert plate

E6000 glue

Something to serve as a base, such as a short-stemmed goblet or an inverted saucer

HOW-TO

Invert the plate. Line the edge of the base that will connect to the plate with a thin ribbon of E6000 glue. Center the glued edge on the underside of the plate. Press firmly and allow to dry completely before turning right side up.

Washing by hand is recommended.

This is truly a one-minute craft and, topped with cookies, makes an easy but impressive last-minute gift. During the year, keep an eye out at garage sales and flea markets for stray pieces of tableware to transform.

CHENILLE CANDY CANES

The earliest known mentions of the candy cane date back to seventeenth-century Europe. A likely scenario for the treat's association with Christmas is that it was sold at holiday fairs, where monks and nuns sold baked goods and sweets to raise money for their orders' annual expenses. The candy may have acquired its hook there, either to associate it with the shepherds of Bethlehem or simply so the pieces could be hung across a pole for display.

When the candy cane arrived in America, it was still all white, as it had been in Europe, and it was not peppermint flavored. One of the earliest mentions of canes as decorations dates back to 1847, when a German-Swedish immigrant named August Imgard hung them from his tree in Wooster, Ohio. It wasn't until the turn of the twentieth century that the candy acquired its iconic red stripe and peppermint flavor. This catapulted the already popular treat to star status, ranking right up there with ribbon candy and homemade fudge as prized treats. Our chenille candy canes are a sweet memory of the first Christmas candy many of us remember.

MATERIALS

1 length of red or green bump chenille, approximately 12 inches (30.5 cm) long

1 length of white bump chenille, approximately 12 inches (30.5 cm) long

Flush cutters or strong kitchen shears

Note: If you are unfamiliar with bump chenille, it's a variation of the plush, fuzzy wired craft stem that resembles a pipe cleaner. Instead of having a uniformly short pile, the chenille swells into plump "bumps" at intervals. Usually, there are three to four bumps per foot (30.5 cm). Bump chenille comes in a variety of colors and is sold in packs of foot-long stems or by the yard or meter.

Line one red and one white chenille stem up so that the bumps on one align with the hollow between the bumps of the other.

Twist together so the stem resembles a barber pole. Trim off any extra stem at the top and bottom with flush cutters. Crimp each end firmly and form a hook at the top.

JULGRANSPLUNDRING

Whenever the candy cane's exact debut as a tree ornament was, it's probable that it was a custom imported from northern Europe, where treats and ginger cookies were more common as tree decorations than in other parts of the world. The Swedes were especially fond of the custom, and they made Christmas last until January 13, St. Knut's Day, by introducing the custom of Julgransplundring, the plundering of the Christmas tree. Adults who find taking down the tree tedious, take note: This is the easy way.

On the appointed day, friends and family gather for one final celebration. Older children are put in charge of removing all but the edible items, and more edibles are added. As the adults look on, drinking coffee and snacking on sweet rolls, the children sing, dance around the tree, and finally are turned loose to plunder the tree, removing all the cookies and wrapped candies and eating to their heart's content. When the tree is finally picked bare, the oldest and strongest boys haul it outside and the oldest girls sweep up the mess.

RUSTIC CANDLE HOLDERS

Taking a pause between the tumultuous 1960s and the country's 1976 bicentennial, America took a long look backward. Previous decades had glanced back nostalgically to Europe, choosing Christmas images from the England of Charles Dickens and Queen Victoria. But in the 1970s, America celebrated its own American past. Laura Ingalls Wilder's series of *Little House on the Prairie* books, first published in the 1930s, became fodder for a top-rated television show, Alex Hailey's bestselling *Roots* opened the door on a hitherto ignored part of the American story, and students in a small Georgia prep school began documenting regional stories and life skills that eventually became the wildly best-selling Foxfire books.

The Foxfire books inspired countless Americans, especially young ones, to try their hand at nearly forgotten arts like quilt making, dulcimer playing, and everything in between. One popular craft to reemerge was punched tin, familiar on pie cabinets but originally used for lanterns before glass was affordable and easy to find. The craft almost certainly came with early European settlers, as punched tin lanterns were used in inns and taverns in Austria, Germany, and other countries. While Paul Revere is typically shown with a glass-sided lantern, punched-tin lanterns were so common that many have argued he was more likely to have carried one of those. Punched–tin can candleholders became a common craft of the early 1970s, and they still cast a cozy vintage glow today.

MATERIALS

Small metal cans, not too much larger than your candles

Terry-cloth towel

Black Sharpie or other water-proof marker

Hammer

Nail large enough to make holes about the size of the head of a pin

Acrylic craft paint

Paintbrush

One 8-inch (20-cm) length 22-gauge wire, or any wire flexible enough to bend easily, per can

Tape

Tracing paper

Plain paper

Rubber bands

HOW-TO

Fill cans with water to within about ½ inch (12 mm) of the top. Set in freezer and let freeze overnight.

Fold the towel and set it on a hard, flat surface, such as a table. Place the frozen can on top. The towel will cushion the can and absorb the moisture as the ice begins to melt.

Do not remove additional cans from the freezer until you are ready to work on them.

CHRISTMAS TREE

Use the Sharpie to sketch the outline of a Christmas tree onto the can.

Make a random pattern of lights within the outline of the tree by hammering the nail in just past the tip to make a small round hole. Pull nail out and repeat.

Finish by making a hole on each side of the can near the top, just below the ice line, marking each end of a diameter line.

Let ice melt and dry can thoroughly.

Paint can with acrylic paint in your choice of colors. Let dry, then give can a second coat.

In a contrasting color, freehand a tree over the holes you made. Start at the top and make short strokes that sweep outward from top to bottom. Broaden the tiers of your tree as you work toward the bottom. Let dry.

Thread the ends of the wire handle through the holes at the top of the can. Twist and bend each end up on the inside to secure.

LITTLE CABIN

Trace the picture on page 140 onto a plain piece of paper and tape into position on the can. Snap two rubber bands around the can, one near the top and one near the bottom, to help hold the image in place.

Condensation from the melting ice will make the paper damp and slippery, so you want to work quickly to make holes at regular intervals as described for the Christmas tree motif. A good approach is to outline the corners of the cabin first and fill in the lines later, after you've done the curving walk.

Finish by making a hole on each side of the can near the top, just below the ice line, marking each end of a diameter line.

Let ice melt and dry can thoroughly.

Paint can with acrylic paint in your choice of colors. Let dry, then give can a second coat.

Thread the ends of the wire handle through the holes at the top of the can. Twist and bend each end up on the inside to secure.

CHENILLE
POINSETTIA GARLAND

The crimson flower that's become synonymous with Christmas owes its name to Joel Poinsett, America's first minister to Mexico, who was so taken with the plant that he brought it back across the border with him in 1825. Despite its long residency, the plant didn't become popular until after 1900, when the Ecke family cultivated a sturdier, showier variety that produced multiple blooms instead of a single flower head. The plant became a favorite Christmas decoration in public spaces such as restaurants and churches. When television became widespread, one of the Ecke sons promoted the plant by sending dozens of poinsettias to television networks to use as set decorations for the many Christmas specials that ran between Thanksgiving and New Year's. He also appeared as a guest on *The Tonight Show*, discussing the plant's beauty and assuring viewers that it was easy to care for and appropriate for the home. That cemented the poinsettia's place as the ultimate Christmas plant, and its popularity has never faded. Today, the poinsettia is the single best-selling potted plant in America, and it accounts for roughly one-quarter of all blooming potted plant sales. Traditional red is the most popular color, but poinsettias also come in shades of pink and cream.

Over the years, artificial poinsettias have been made of everything from construction paper and crepe paper to felt, wax, plastic, wire-strung seed beads, and chenille. Our chenille version is very much like the ones that were popular in the 1940s and '50s.

Tape

String

Bump chenille sold by the yard
(see Measure Swag and
Calculate Chenille, below)

Yellow double-tipped floral
stamens, 3 pieces for each
poinsettia

24-gauge wire or thin, flexible
twist tie–weight wire

Artificial greenery swag
(see Measure Swag and
Calculate Chenille, below)

Red double tipped berries

HOW-TO

MEASURE SWAG AND CALCULATE CHENILLE

Tape the string to where you plan to hang your garland, adding to the ends if you want extra length on each side and adjusting the center to get the depth of swag you want. Measure string to find out how long your garland should be.

To calculate how much chenille to buy, you will need to know how many bumps the chenille has per yard (see note on page 78). Each poinsettia has 7 leaves, and each leaf requires 2 bumps, so you need 14 bumps per poinsettia. We used chenille that had approximately 10 bumps per yard and anchored the centers of our poinsettias to the garland at 9-inch (23-cm) intervals. If you used shorter bumps and your flowers are smaller, you will want to space them at more frequent intervals.

MAKE THE GARLAND

To form each petal, bend the thin section between 2 bumps in half. Pinch together to form the tip of a petal. Wrap the raw end of the first bump around the base of the second to hold in place.

Do not cut chenille, but make 6 more petals in a continuous piece. If it helps you shape the flower, you can hook 1 or 2 petals together at the base by wrapping the base of one over the base of a petal opposite. When you have completed 7 petals,

cut the length of chenille at the thin spot after the last petal and wrap the end around the base of the petal.

Gather 3 double-tipped stamens together. Fold the bundle in half so all 6 tips are together and there's a loop on the other end. Secure the bundle with a 5-inch (12-cm) length of wire, leaving about 2 inches (5 cm) of wire free on each end.

Thread the wire through the inner points of the petals, drawing them together. As you do this, push the stamen bundle into the center of the flower so just the tips show and the loop protrudes through the back of the flower. Pull the wire tight to bury it in the pile of the chenille and secure the petals. Thread one end of the wire through the loop of the stamens. Trim the ends of the wire to a few inches or centimeters long each, which you will use to secure the poinsettia to the swag.

Make the number of poinsettias needed for your swag. As you attach them to the greenery swag, bend and position the petals to balance each poinsettia and show it to its best advantage.

To finish, wrap the double-tipped berries into the greenery garland between the poinsettias.

SPARKLING
CHRISTMAS TREES

How did the pine tree, and not Bethlehem's palm, become the emblematic tree of the holiday season? Throughout pagan Europe, the winter solstice was celebrated to mark the passing of winter's cold, short days, and plants that retained their year-round green were used to decorate homes and temples. As Christianity replaced paganism, the old customs remained, and the year-round green of holly and other plants became symbolic of life everlasting. The practice of having decorated trees in the home originated in sixteenth-century Germany and, though German immigrants brought the tradition to America with them, Puritan descendants looked on it as a pagan holdover. Only in the late 1840s did Christmas trees finally become widely accepted.

Once established, the Christmas tree became one of the holiday's most popular symbols. In addition to full-size trees, small artificial trees have adorned tables and mantels for more than a hundred years. Made of feathers, cotton, cellophane, bottlebrush, nylon netting, chenille, cloth, ceramic, ribbon, straw, and just about anything else, they've been a favorite with crafters over the years. A cluster of Traditional Trees, pictured here, makes a classic retro mantel decoration or tablescape, while an elongated, triangular Modern Tree is reminiscent of the streamlined designs of the 1960s, especially when done in atomic shades like platinum, white, ice blue, chartreuse, or vibrant turquoise.

MATERIALS

Tracing paper

Pencil

Craft knife or very sharp, fine-pointed scissors

Ruler

Tape

2 pieces lightweight cardboard such as from cracker or cereal boxes for each tree

Scotch Positionable Mounting Adhesive

Brayer or rolling pin

Several sheets of clean, unused printer paper

Glitter in your choice of colors

HOW-TO

To make Traditional Trees, fold tracing paper lengthwise and place the fold along the center line of the pattern on page 140. Trace and cut out the pattern of the size tree you want. Make a midpoint mark on each pattern.

To make Modern Trees, fold a piece of tracing paper in half lengthwise. Decide how tall you want the tree to be and make a dot where the tip will be, measuring from the bottom edge of the paper. Decide how wide you want the base to be and make a mark half that length at the bottom edge, measuring from the fold. Use a ruler to connect the dot marking the tip of the tree to the dot marking the base. Cut along the line, open the paper, and you will have an elegantly modern looking tree pattern. Mark the midpoint along the fold.

Once you have created your pattern for either the Traditional or Modern tree, tape pattern to cardboard, trace, and cut out 2 cardboard pieces for each tree you want to make. Mark the center point on each cardboard piece. Use the ruler to draw a straight line from tip of the tree down through the center point all the way to the base. Cut one piece along the line from the top down to the center point, and the other piece along the line from the bottom up to the center point.

Working with one piece at a time, cut a section of mounting adhesive large enough to cover the piece. Position it over the cutout tree with the exposed sticky side down and the protective liner up. Press down firmly, smoothing with your hands. It's important to get good and complete coverage, so go over it with a brayer or rolling pin. Turn tree over and cover the other side with mounting adhesive in the same way.

Use a craft knife or small sharp scissors to cut away excess mounting paper, trimming as close to the edges of the tree as possible. Cut through the liner papers along the slit you made in the tree piece.

Peel away the protective liner on one side and lay the piece, sticky side up, on a sheet of clean paper. Pour glitter over the piece, covering it completely. Lay a second piece of paper over the top and press down firmly, going over the surface with your hands, a brayer, or rolling pin to really push the glitter into the sticky surface.

Allow to set a few minutes, then tap off excess glitter. Place piece glittered side down on a fresh piece of paper, peel off adhesive liner, and repeat.

Apply glitter to the second piece as you did the first. Occasionally, there may be a spot where the glitter did not stick. These can be touched up by applying a drop of glue to the bare spot and covering with glitter. Return unused glitter to the container. Allow pieces to cure several hours.

Assemble tree by sliding the slotted pieces together and arranging them at right angles. If the slits are too tight to let the pieces stand at right angles, carefully trim a tiny strip from the inside of the slot and reassemble.

BEJEWELED BALLS

The mid-nineteeth century was a turning point for Christmas ornaments. Glass ornaments had long been an artisanal cottage industry, with whole families working nearly around the clock to create and hand paint ornaments that brought meager earnings. Then, a method of making brighter and shinier ornaments while eliminating much of the laborious handwork was introduced. The product that made this method possible was known as mercury glass.

Where silvered paint, applied by hand, had previously been the only way to make an ornament glisten, the new process created items with a double wall of glass and a narrow space between. Silver paint, or colors made shinier with the addition of silvering, was then flowed into the narrow space. The outer layer of glass added a luster like no other, and the demand for ornaments soared. In addition to round ornaments, the new technique could be adapted to make molded ornaments, and this resulted in one of the most popular items in Christmas history: the reflector ball. A classic reflector is round or teardrop shaped, with a conical depression molded into a design radiating from the center. While the ornament itself might be any color, the indented design was most often done in brightest silver for maximum dazzle.

Sadly, reflector balls are largely a collector's item these days, and we have yet to think of a way to craft an acceptable facsimile. But if you can't go concave, why not go convex? Our Bejeweled Balls add a bit of vintage sparkle and take just minutes to make.

MATERIALS

An assortment of costume jewelry earrings, pins and settings, rhinestone shank-style buttons, or similar trinkets

Plastic safety glasses

Jewelry clippers

E6000 glue

2½-inch (6-cm) Christmas ball ornaments in glass or plastic, colors of your choice

Beads or small fish sinkers (optional)

Gold or silver spray paint (optional)

Narrow ribbon or cord to make hangers

HOW-TO

Raid your junk jewelry drawer, button box, local thrift shops, dollar stores, and eBay for cheap costume jewelry glitz. (We found that searching "earrings" and "pins" on eBay and sorting to display least expensive items first gave us endless choices before we even went as high as a dime.) Wearing safety glasses, use jewelry clippers to snip off backings and clip-on clasps from your jewels. Remove ear wires and unnecessary jump rings and connectors. You only want the essential components, with as flat a back as possible.

Glue jewels to balls with E6000 glue. Let set.

Depending on how heavy the jewel is, it may affect the ball's balance, and you will want to correct this. There are two ways this can be done. If you are working with earrings, you can glue the second earring to the opposite side of the ball. If you only have one earring or a single pin, you can make a counterweight.

To make a counterweight, choose one or two beads that together are about the same weight of the component. If you attached a very heavy component, such as a pin, you can use a fish sinker spray-painted gold or silver. Attach the beads or sinker to ribbons and tie the ribbon to the ornament loop at the top so the weight falls to the middle of the ball on the opposite side of the jewel.

Cut 6-inch (15-cm) lengths of narrow ribbon to make hangers for the ornaments.

FANTASY BIRDS

Like many Christmas traditions, the practice of putting birds on trees began in Germany. Early ornaments were inspired by nature and often whittled from wood. It would have seemed natural to add bird figures to the fruits and nuts already on the tree. Not only were birds a harbinger of spring, they were also seen as messengers of good news. Since the fifth century, the dove had been used in mosaics and paintings, including those depicting the Annunciation, to symbolize the Holy Spirit.

When Germany's cottage glassblowing industry began producing tree ornaments in the sixteenth century, birds were one of the most in-demand ornaments. Unfortunately, they were also one of the most difficult to create, and only a few families had glassblowers skilled enough to specialize in bird ornaments.

F. W. Woolworth began importing glass birds to the United States for sale in his stores in the 1880s. If anything, the ornaments were even more popular than they had been in Europe. Birds were already a favorite motif of the sentimental Victorians, to whom they also symbolized love and romance. Among the myriad ornaments imported by Woolworth, birds reigned supreme, challenged only by the ever-popular reflector balls.

Unless you're lucky enough to have inherited several of these scarce ornaments, building a collection to trim a tree would be time consuming and costly—but anyone can load their branches with a flock of Fantasy Birds like the ones shown here.

MATERIALS FOR EACH BIRD

One 1½-inch (4-cm) Styrofoam ball, for body

Straight pins

Scissors

One 1-inch (25-cm) Styrofoam ball, for head

Safety glasses

1½-inch (4-cm) head pins

Jewelry clippers

E6000 glue

Toothpicks or bamboo skewers

Small piece of brown felt for beaks

Ruler

Two 1-inch (2.5-cm) eye pins (or longer eye pins, trimmed to 1 inch [2.5 cm])

Cord or clear nylon string for hanging

FOR BROWN BIRD

Terrifically Tacky Tape, ¼ inch (6mm) wide

2 yards (1.8 m) of 8-mm bronze string sequins for body

1 yard (.9 m) of 5-mm brown string sequins for head

Pheasant feathers, 1 to 3 inches (2.5 to 7.5 cm) long for wings

Light blue marabou feathers, any length to trim wings and tail

2 brown and cream feather picks, 5 inches (12 cm) long, or assorted brown and cream feathers, 3 to 5 inches (7.5 to 12 cm) long, for tail

Two 3-mm light-blue beads or faux pearls for eyes

FOR PINK BIRD

Mod Podge

Paintbrush

Shallow bowl

Pink matte embossing powder

Guinea feathers for wings, 1 to

3½ inches (2.5 to 9 cm) long

Pink marabou feathers for tail, 4 to 6 inches (10 to 15 cm) long

Two 5-mm brown sequins or beads for eyes

Begin by making the body of the bird, using the larger Styrofoam ball and the bronze sequins. To begin, wind the tacky tape once around the ball in a belt that divides the ball in half. Press the tape firmly so that it adheres to the ball. Don't remove the liner, but peel it back a bit so the end of the tape can cover the starting point, and you have 2 tabs of liner. Now make a second belt that begins and ends where the first one did, and divides the ball into 4 even sections. Make 2 more belts so that you end up with a ball that's divided into 8 sections, like an orange. The bands should crisscross each other at the "north pole" (where you began) and at the "south pole," directly opposite it. At the north pole you should have 8 tabs of liner that have been peeled back from the tape.

Set the ball aside and take up the string of sequins. Use a pin to unlace the threads and slide off 3 or 4 sequins. Don't cut the thread or let it get tangled—the purpose of this is to give you long enough ends of thread to knot. When you have enough thread to tie, make a double knot and trim the thread ends.

Pull back 1 inch (2.5 cm) or so of liner on all 8 liners to expose the tape. Use straight pins to pin the liners to the ball to hold them out of your way as you work.

Press the end of the sequin string to the center of the north pole, pressing it firmly to the crisscrossed tape. Now begin wrapping the ball in a spiral, making sure the top of the row you are laying down overlaps the bottom of the row above. If you do go a bit off course, lift the sequin string and reposition it. Continue peeling back liner and wrapping sequin string, pressing sequins down firmly as you go.

When you get to the bottom, trim as much of the liner off as possible. After the last sequin is in place, cut the sequin string, leaving about 1 inch (2.5 cm) of extra sequins. As you did at the top, gently unthread some sequins to give yourself enough thread to knot. Tie and trim off the extra thread. Repeat with the 1-inch (2.5-cm) Styrofoam ball to make the head.

When you attach the head to the body, the balls should be arranged so that each row of sequins overlaps the row behind it.

Wearing safety glasses, snip the end off a head pin using jewelry clippers. Dip pin into the E6000 glue about ½ inch (12 mm) deep, then slide into the head. Let set a minute or two, then dip the free end of the pin into glue and slide it into the body. Use a toothpick to dab some E6000 glue into the spot where the head and body meet and press firmly together. Let set.

While the head and body are drying, build the wings. Unlike the pink bird, whose wings are flat to the body, this bird's wings are extended in flight. Pick out 2 or 3 pheasant feathers—1 longer one and 1 or 2 shorter ones, and a piece of blue marabou feather for each wing. Try to pick matching sets for each side, so the wings will be similar in size. Clip off the bottom of the shaft if the feathers are sparse there.

Layer each wing with the largest feather on the bottom, the blue marabou feather on top, then the smaller feathers on top of the marabou. Wispy bits of blue marabou should just peek out between the brown. When you are satisfied with the way the feathers look, use E6000 glue to attach them together at the base. Set aside to dry.

While the wings are drying, build the tail fan in the same way, using feather picks or brown and cream feathers of different lengths. Glue together at the base and set aside to dry.

Use E6000 glue to attach the upper half of a straight pin to the underside of each wing, placing the pin alongside the shaft. Make sure the bottom (sharp) half of the pin protrudes beyond the base of the wing. When pins are dry, dip the free end of a pin in E6000 glue and attach the wing by working the pin between the sequins and sliding it into the bird's body.

When the tail is dry, glue the base, upright, directly over the spot where the sequin spiral ends.

Trim a marabou feather to make a fluffy 2-inch (5-cm) piece and glue to the back side of the tail with a dab of E6000 glue.

Wearing safety glasses, snip two straight pins or head pins ½ inch (12 mm) from the head of the pin. Thread a blue bead onto each and slide into head to make the eyes.

To make the bird's beak, cut a ¼-by-½-inch (6-by-12-mm) diamond shape from the brown felt. Fold in half at the short centerline. Set something heavy on the folded piece for several minutes. Attach beak by sliding a straight pin through the middle of the crease and into the head.

Finish by working an eye pin between the sequins into the top center of the body about ½ inch (12 mm) from the head. Thread the nylon string through the loop and tie to make a hanging loop.

PINK BIRD

Paint the ball for the head with Mod Podge, then hold over shallow bowl and pour on pink embossing powder. Drop the head into the bowl and use a toothpick to roll it around until it is thoroughly coated. Let dry a few minutes, then gently lift with the toothpick, shake off excess powder, and set aside to dry thoroughly.

Repeat process with the body.

While the head and body are drying, build the wings. Pick out 2 or 3 guinea feathers for each wing—1 longer one and 1 or 2 shorter ones. Try to pick similar sets for each side, so the wings will be similar in size.

Layer the wings with the largest piece on the bottom, slightly fanned and right side up. They should form a wing shape and be mirror images of each other. Use a toothpick to dab on E6000 glue to attach them together at the forward end of the wing. Set aside to dry.

Wearing safety glasses, snip the end off a head pin using jewelry clippers. Dip pin into the E6000 glue about ½ inch (12 mm) deep, then slide into head. Let set a minute or two, then dip the free end of the pin into glue and slide into the body. Use a toothpick to dab some E6000 into the spot where the head and body meet and press firmly together. Let set.

Position wings by pinning lightly in place. Adjust as needed, then glue the forward third of each wing (the section nearest the head) to the body, leaving the rest of the wing free. Unlike the brown bird, the pink bird's wings should look folded to the body.

Choose two pink marabou feathers for the tail. Clip off the bottom of the shaft if the feathers are sparse there—you want the base of the tail to be nice and plumey. Use E6000 glue to attach the upper half of a straight pin to the underside of the base of the tail, placing the pin alongside the shaft. Make sure the bottom (sharp) half of the pin protrudes beyond the base of the tail. Do this to both tail feathers. When pins are dry, dip the free end of each pin in E6000 glue and drive into the bird's body horizontally to form the tail.

Wearing safety glasses, snip two straight pins or head pins ½ inch (12 mm) from the head. Thread a brown sequin onto each and slide into head to make the eyes.

To make the bird's beak, cut a ¼-by-½-inch (6-by-12-mm) diamond shape from the brown felt. Fold in half at the short centerline. Set something heavy on the folded piece for several minutes. Attach beak by sliding a straight pin through the middle of the crease and into the head.

Finish by sliding an eye pin into the top center of the body about ½ inch (12 mm) from the head. Thread the cord or nylon string through the eye and tie to make a hanging loop.

PARTY INVITATIONS

Christmas was originally a rather quiet holiday in the United States, a day of calm spiritual reflection to be spent with close family. In addition to the Puritan tradition of solemnity, it's likely that the geography of the country itself contributed to the lack of mass gatherings. The U.S. is large, and in a time when many people lived on the frontier or, later, on farms across a vast landscape, travel was a daunting prospect. As the country filled with cities and people, Christmas became less solemn and far more social. By the late 1800s, people were inviting friends to tree-trimming parties. Fifty years later, Christmas cocktail parties were all the rage. These days, the air is filled with calls of "We must get together over the holidays"—and all too quickly our schedules fill up. Why not turn the clock back and take a tip from our parents and grandparents? Whether it's a tree-trimming party, a cocktail soiree, or a potluck buffet, getting together with the people you like the best is really what the holiday is about.

Or maybe you'd rather host a New Year's Eve party, that ultimate emblem of the swanky suburban lifestyle that grew out of World War II. Previous generations had made the night a bigger blast with each passing year of the twentieth century. If you were young and carefree at the turn of the century, you might spend the evening at a rooftop garden restaurant. In the '20s and '30s, the hot venue might be a nightclub, a ballroom with a big band blasting away, or the local country club. After the war, people found they could have just as much fun at home, especially when those homes sported bars, hi-fi systems, rumpus rooms, and, eventually, color television.

Since New Year's is the time for putting on the Ritz, why not welcome it with a retro-theme party? Pick your favorite decade, ask your guests to dress in the spirit, and set the mood by using our vintage images to make your own invitations.

MATERIALS

Notecards and envelopes, size A-1 or similar

Confetti in Christmas or New Year's themes

Pop Dots, any size, or double-sided Scotch tape

HOW-TO

Make copies of the images below or on page 105 and then cut and attach to outside and inside of notecards with Pop Dots or double-sided tape.

Slide a notecard into each envelope with the spine down, and drop a spoonful of confetti into the card before sealing the envelope.

Come to Our Party!

When _____

Where _____

what are you doing
new year's eve?

Come Join Us

time & date _____

the place to be _____

HOLIDAY DRINK CHARMS

When sixteen million GIs returned from World War II, there were millions of marriages, and the sudden boom in birth rate, led to a housing shortage of historic proportions. Newlyweds bunked with parents or rented one-room city apartments with Murphy beds and hot plates that passed for a kitchen. Housing outside the city limits was too expensive, and construction was too slow to alleviate the problem until Levitt & Sons, a real estate and construction company, came along and applied the techniques of mass production to housing. Levittown, New York, became the first modern American suburb, where a veteran could buy his own ranch home for $7,990 by putting down a $90 deposit and making payments of $58 a month. Other developers followed suit, and suburbs blossomed, seemingly overnight, from coast to coast.

The migration from city and farm to the suburbs changed almost everything about America. Suddenly, houses included never-before-seen spaces with modern-sounding names like "rumpus room" and "rec room." Where New Year's Eve was once celebrated at a club downtown, now one had friends and neighbors over. One of the first improvements a suburban homeowner was likely to add was a home bar, a luxury previously present only in the homes of the very wealthy and the Hollywood glamour set. The bar, of course, necessitated not only booze but bar stools, an array of special glasses, bar gear, and perhaps a blender or an ice crusher. And once the basics were in place, manufacturers thought of extras—coasters, ice buckets, fancy swizzle sticks, drink socks, and cocktail napkins. The old practice of marking someone's glass with a name written on masking tape was out of place amidst such swank. Drink charms were inevitable.

8 gold or silver hoop earrings, 1 inch (2.5 cm) in diameter

Chain-nose and round-nose jewelry pliers

2 green and 1 red plastic holly leaf charms, approximately 18 mm long

Jump rings

1 red shank button

1 glass or plastic ring link in green or white, approximately 20 mm in diameter

Red alcohol ink or Sharpie pen

2 lightweight, bendable silver 4-pronged bead caps

1 small gold bead

1 large round green bead, approximately 24 mm in diameter

Head pins

Jewelry clippers

Safety glasses

1 silver snowflake charm

7 light-blue or pale-aqua crystals, 4 mm size

1 Santa head charm

1 round red bead, 1 round green bead, 6 mm size

Alphabet beads that spell out CHEERS, drilled side to side

2 round bright-aqua beads, 6 mm size

1 triangular green bead, about 1 inch (2.5 cm) long, drilled top to bottom

2 round light-blue opaque beads, 8 mm size

HOW-TO

If your hoops have one end bent to catch in the eye of the other end, straighten the bend with the pliers before threading on charms and beads. After adding charms and beads on each hoop, bend the end at an angle so it will catch and hold in the eye of the hoop.

Green Holly Leaves and Berry: Fit each green holly leaf with a jump ring and close. Thread both jump rings into a third jump ring, thread the ring through the button shank, and close. Thread the button shank onto the hoop.

Red Holly Leaf Dangle: Thread a red holly leaf onto a jump ring, thread jump ring onto a ring link, and close. Thread ring link onto a second jump ring (opposite the holly leaf) and close. Thread jump ring onto hoop.

Green Globe Bead: Using alcohol ink or a Sharpie, color a silver bead cap red on the side that will show. Thread the small gold bead onto a head pin. Thread on the bead cap, tinted side down. Thread the large green bead onto a head pin. Form a loop and crimp closed with pliers, clipping off any excess head pin. Holding charm upside down, press the arms of the bead cap down over the green bead so that, when turned right side up, the four red-tinted arms are cupping the green bead. Thread loop onto the hoop.

Snowflake Dangle: Thread a jump ring through the loop of the snowflake charm and close ring. Thread 3 blue crystals onto hoop, thread on the jump ring of the snowflake charm, then thread on 3 additional crystals.

Santa Head: Thread round red bead onto a head pin, add Santa head, form loop, close, and clip off excess. Thread loop onto hoop.

Cheers: Thread 1 aqua bead onto hoop, thread on the CHEERS beads, thread on remaining aqua bead.

Christmas Tree: Thread 1 round green bead onto a head pin, thread 1 triangular green bead on, pointed end up. Form loop, close, and clip off excess. Thread loop onto hoop.

Blue and Silver Fountain: Thread a light-blue or pale aqua crystal onto a head pin. Thread on a silver bead cap, right side down. Thread on the 2 round light-blue opaque beads. Form loop and crimp closed with pliers, clipping off any excess head pin. Holding charm upside down, press the arms of the bead cap down over the blue beads so that, when turned right side up, the 4 arms are cupping the beads. Thread loop onto the hoop.

NEW YEAR'S PARTY HAT

There are two theories about the origins of the party hat. One dates back to ancient civilizations, where shamans, wise men, and seers were often the only ones permitted to wear special hats.

An alternative theory, which makes more sense, focuses on the tall, cone-shaped dunce's cap, once forced on students to shame them for their foolish behavior and unwillingness to learn. Early party hats were almost invariably mini dunce caps—small cones decorated in bright colors and topped with tissue-paper pompoms. Advertisements and illustrations from the era often show birthday celebrations with just one person, the birthday boy or girl, wearing the hat. Rather than a sense of shame, the hat conveyed special status to the guest of honor, giving the wearer license to act frivolous and ignore the responsibilities he would otherwise have. From here it was only a hop, skip, and jump to the custom of wearing hats on New Year's Eve, a night when everyone had a free pass to revelry.

New Year's party hats quickly diversified. By the 1920s, fez-type hats appeared, no doubt inspired by the 1922 discovery of King Tut's tomb and the new attention paid to North Africa.

Also popular in the 1920s and '30s were hats like the one in this project: send-ups of the Victorian smoking hat, worn by men at home in their leisure and more elaborately by women with winter coats. The hat was pillbox-shaped and had either a flat or domed top with a tassel anchored at the center. This hat can be worn with the dome lifted or flattened.

Two 11-by-2-inch (28-by-5-cm) pieces of flexible, lightweight cardboard

Terrifically Tacky Tape or stapler with staples

Sheet-style crepe paper, 2 colors for each hat you want to make

Bone folder or heavy table knife

Wired tinsel craft stems in colors of your choice

Scissors

Glue dots

Confetti

HOW-TO

Overlap the cardboard pieces by ¼ inch (6 mm) and secure them by putting a strip of tape between them or stapling them together at both ends to form a circle.

Cut a piece of crepe paper that measures 20 by 23 inches (50 by 58 cm) for the body of the hat. Make sure the grain of the paper runs parallel to the short side.

Cut a piece of contrasting crepe paper that measures 3½ by 23 inches (9 by 58 cm), with the grain of the paper parallel to the short side.

Place the contrasting paper on top of one of the 23-inch (58-cm) ends so the edges are even with each other. Attach it to the larger piece along the bottom edge, leaving both pieces free at the top of the 23-inch (58-cm) edge, at intervals using 1-inch (2.5-cm) long strips of tape or staples.

Fold in half by bringing the opposite 23-inch (58-cm) edge down to the first and pressing to make a firm fold. The contrasting paper should be between the two main colors. Use a bone folder or the handle of a heavy table knife to make the crease as sharp as possible. You should now have a folded piece that measures 10 by 23 inches (25 by 58 cm).

Turn one of the 10-inch (25-cm) edges under about ⅜ inch (1 cm) and press firmly.

Position the fold of the 23-inch (58-cm) edge to cover just the lower edge of the cardboard band with the contrasting paper edge at the top. Attach the raw 10-inch (25-cm) edge to the band with tape.

Secure the folded 23-inch (58-cm) edge all the way around the bottom of the hat band, using 2-inch (5-cm) sections of tape at 2-inch (5-cm) intervals. Overlap the folded short edge and secure it to the raw edge all the way to the top with more sections of tape.

Gather the top of the hat about 3½ inches (9 cm) down, aiming to position it at the center of the circle. Pinch it together as firmly as possible and secure it with a wired tinsel craft stem. Add a second stem for extra hold.

Create a pompom by cutting from the top down at ¼-inch (6-mm) intervals along the top. Fluff the fringe so that both colors show.

Use glue dots to decorate the hat with pieces of confetti.

Finally, twist the ends of the craft sticks into fancy swirls.

Now you're ready to party!

Butter Coins, page 125

The Twelve

Days of Christmas

Cookie Swap

Cookie swaps are a thoroughly American, thoroughly twentieth-century invention. Early references that date from World War I are somewhat misleading, as the "cookie exchanges" publicized in local newspapers were fund-raising events, better known today as bake sales. The cookie exchange as we know it, where each guest brings a set number of cookies for every other guest and goes home with a broad selection of treats, seems to have come into its own after World War II, probably as an outgrowth of the new suburban lifestyle and another of its traditions, the neighborhood coffee party.

Newspaper notices and references to true cookie swaps began to appear in the early 1950s, and within a decade they were an established trend. To feed the new tradition, newspaper food sections and women's magazines expanded the number of Christmas cookie recipes, taking the cookie tradition far beyond sugar cookies and gingerbread men. One of the country's most famous swaps, the Wellesley Cookie Exchange, begun in 1971 and still going strong, received so many recipe requests following an article in *Yankee* magazine that the group published its own cookbook in 1986.

Despite the fact that we're supposed to be busier and more sugar-shy than ever, the cookie exchange tradition continues, and swaps thrive in neighborhoods and clubs across the country. Here are a dozen easy-to-make recipes, one for each of the Twelve Days of Christmas and none requiring time-consuming rolling out or decorating.

RUSSIAN TEA CAKES

Ground nuts, ground grain, and a sweetener such as sugar or honey constitute one of the oldest and most universal of pastry doughs, found centuries ago in Egypt and the Middle East and later in Europe from England to Lithuania and beyond. The modern version is based on a treat served in eighteenth-century Russia as part of a tea service. Because the recipe makes the most of butter and sugar, uses no eggs, and features nuts, which many people grew and harvested in their own yards, the recipe may have gotten a popularity boost during World War II, when rationing and food shortages influenced holiday baking. A traditional offering at weddings in Mexico, these rich but not-too-sweet cookies are also known as Mexican Wedding Cakes, Butterballs, and Snowballs. Although early versions called for walnuts or pecans, we have seen recent recipes calling for almonds, cashews, hazelnuts, and even pistachios.

Makes 2 dozen cookies

INGREDIENTS

½ cup (115 g) unsalted butter, at room temperature

¼ cup (25 g) confectioners' sugar, plus more for rolling

½ teaspoon pure vanilla extract

1 cup plus 2 tablespoons (143 g) all-purpose flour

½ teaspoon salt

½ cup finely ground pecans or walnuts

HOW-TO

1. Cream butter, sugar, and vanilla with an electric mixer until smooth and creamy, scraping down bowl to make sure all of the butter is incorporated.

2. Add flour and salt and mix until just combined.

3. With a rubber spatula, stir in nuts until fully incorporated.

4. Chill dough in the refrigerator until stiff enough to roll into 1-inch (2.5-cm)

balls, about one hour. Once chilled and shaped, preheat the oven to 350°F (175°C). Place balls about 2 inches (5 cm) apart on a cookie sheet lined with parchment paper.

5. Bake on the middle rack of the oven for 10 to 12 minutes, until edges of cookies are lightly browned.

6. While cookies are still warm, roll in confectioners' sugar to thoroughly coat tops and sides. Finish cooling completely before storing.

GINGER COOKIES

How did a spice of the ancient Mediterranean, used by Greeks and Romans, make its way into the signature Christmas cookie of the West? We owe it to the Persians, who invented the first recognizable ancestor of the cookie and used a vast array of spices in their cuisine. Although the introduction of gingerbread to Europe is often attributed to returning Crusaders, it was actually introduced by an Armenian monk, Saint Gregory Makar, who emigrated to France in 992 and spent the last years of his life teaching fellow monks how to make the pastry. Over the years, gingerbread production became a source of income for religious orders across Europe. The product was so wildly popular that gingerbread fairs were a common feature of medieval holidays, and gingerbread tied with a colorful ribbon was the equivalent of today's heart-shaped box of chocolates. In addition to its piquant flavor, gingerbread's stiff dough lent itself to artistic creation; it could be shaped into swans, animals, flowers, figures, and other fanciful shapes and decorated with raisins and plain white frosting. Queen Elizabeth I once impressed foreign visitors by serving gingerbread baked in her own likeness. While gingerbread men remain a symbolic favorite, they are fussy to make and are often dry. For ease of baking and ginger-laden goodness, we opt for the recipe here.

Makes 3½ to 4 dozen cookies

INGREDIENTS

¾ cup (170 g) unsalted butter, at room temperature

1 cup (200 g) granulated sugar, plus more for rolling

1 large egg

½ cup (120 ml) light or "original" molasses (not blackstrap)

1½ teaspoons baking soda

1 teaspoon cinnamon

1 teaspoon ginger

1 teaspoon salt

½ teaspoon ground cloves

2 cups (255 g) all-purpose flour

HOW-TO

1. Cream butter and sugar with an electric mixer until light and fluffy, scraping down bowl to make sure all of the butter is incorporated.

2. Mix in egg and molasses and stir until combined.

3. In a separate bowl, whisk together dry ingredients. Add to cookie mixture and mix until just incorporated.

4. Chill dough until stiff enough to shape into 1-inch (2.5-cm) balls, about one hour. Once chilled and shaped, preheat oven to 350°F (175°C). Roll the balls in sugar and place on a cookie sheet lined with parchment paper. Bake on middle rack of the oven for 8 to 10 minutes. How long you bake these cookies depends on your personal preference. If you bake them longer, a bit over 10 minutes, you will have crisp gingersnaps. Baked just for 8 minutes, they retain a soft, chewy, almost candylike center.

MACAROONS

Macaroons originated more than a thousand years ago in the monasteries of Italy as a small, crisp cookie made from egg whites and finely ground almonds or almond paste. Since monasteries and convents baked breads and pastries to earn money at holiday times, the cookie quickly became a Christmas favorite. Among the many gifts Catherine de Medici brought to the French court when she married King Henri II were her pastry chefs, and soon the macaroon was popular throughout France. For some it became, quite literally, a life-saving treat—two Benedictine nuns, seeking asylum from the terrors of the Revolution, fled to the small town of Nancy and survived by baking and selling the cookie. Over time, coconut was added to the recipe, and in many areas it replaced the ground almonds completely. Throughout the United States, Britain, and Australia, the coconut macaroon is more common than any other type, though recently the pastel-tinted, crème-filled, sandwich-style French version has become popular. The recipe given here is for the deliciously light, flourless type popular from the 1930s on.

Makes about 20 cookies

INGREDIENTS

2 large egg whites, at room temperature

Small pinch of salt

A few drops of almond extract, or more to taste

¼ cup (50 g) granulated sugar

1⅓ cups (120 g) sweetened coconut, shredded or flaked

HOW-TO

1. Preheat oven to 350°F (175°C).

2. In an electric mixer, beat the eggs whites with salt on medium-high until they begin to stiffen.

3. Add almond extract and about one-third of the sugar and continue to whip on high. Add another third of the sugar while continuing to beat, then add remaining sugar.

4. Whip until egg whites hold a stiff peak. Use a rubber spatula to fold in coconut until fully incorporated.

5. Drop by teaspoonful on a cookie sheet lined with parchment paper, leaving about 2 inches (5 cm) between each cookie.

6. Bake on middle rack of oven 15 to 20 minutes, until the outside is light golden brown. Cool completely before storing. These are best made in small batches and eaten within a few days, when the exteriors are still crisp.

LACE COOKIES

This candylike cookie with nuts and brown sugar is claimed by many countries, including Italy, France, and Belgium. An early, decidedly humble American version used oatmeal rather than nuts and is often referred to as Irish Lace. The confection got a major upgrade in 1957, when *Gourmet* magazine published a recipe that used ground almonds rather than oatmeal. The cookie quickly became a favorite with hostesses who wanted something delicate and sophisticated for holiday entertaining.

Makes about 3 dozen cookies

INGREDIENTS

3 tablespoons (43 g) unsalted butter

½ cup (110 g) packed light brown sugar

¼ cup (60 ml) light corn syrup

⅓ cup (40 g) all-purpose flour

½ teaspoon pure vanilla extract

½ cup (45 g) coarsely chopped toasted almonds

1. Preheat oven to 350°F (175°C).

2. Combine butter, sugar, and corn syrup in a medium-sized saucepan and heat over medium-low heat, stirring occasionally. When sugar is dissolved and the mixture is completely combined, remove from heat.

3. Using a heatproof rubber spatula, stir in flour and vanilla until combined. Add almonds and stir again until combined.

4. To bake, line a cookie sheet with a silicone mat or parchment paper and drop by teaspoonful, leaving 3 inches (7.5 cm) between each cookie. Bake on middle rack of oven 6 to 8 minutes, just until golden brown. The centers of the cookies will not be set. Cool completely before storing.

5. There are several ways to serve this cookie, the most traditional of which are to leave them flat or to wrap them around a wooden broom handle or dowel while they are still warm and pliant, forming a tube that can be left hollow or filled with sweetened whipped cream just before serving. They can also be pressed into a muffin tin to form small bowls for ice cream. To serve the cookies flat, let cool on the sheet until they are firm enough to transfer. If you are shaping them and find they have become too rigid, the cookies can be returned to the oven for a few moments.

VARIATIONS

There are many variations of this cookie, including Lady Bird Johnson's, which substitutes ½ cup (45 g) shredded coconut for the almonds. Belgian Lace cookies are topped with a drizzle of semisweet chocolate, while the Florentine Lace version adds both orange zest to the batter and a finishing drizzle of chocolate atop the baked cookie.

PECAN TASSIES

The likely origin of the name "tassie" is France, since these miniature tarts are baked in a cup-like pastry shell and the French word for cup is *tasse*. Further speculation holds that, since sugared almonds were a popular ingredient in many French confections, French immigrants to the American South substituted plentiful local pecans for almonds to re-create many traditional treats, including pralines as well as the immediate ancestor of tassies, pecan pie. Despite their long-standing origins, many Americans think of Pecan Tassies as a relatively new cookie, particularly in northern states. The first known mention of them dates to an article in the *Los Angeles Times* in January 1968. Since virtually all recipes for pecan tassies call for cream cheese in the crust, it's likely that the tassie as we know it came about between the introduction of Philadelphia Cream Cheese in 1928 and the newspaper article in 1968.

Makes 2 dozen tarts

For this recipe you will need a mini muffin tin and paper liners

INGREDIENTS

For the pastry shells:

½ cup (115 g) unsalted butter, at room temperature

3 ounces (85 g) cream cheese, at room temperature

1 cup (130 g) all-purpose flour

For the filling:

¾ cup (165 g) packed light brown sugar

1 large egg

1 teaspoon pure vanilla extract

1 cup (110 g) chopped toasted pecans, plus two dozen unbroken pecan halves

1. For the pastry shells: Cream butter and cream cheese with an electric mixer until smooth, scraping down bowl to make sure the two are thoroughly combined.

2. Mix in flour until combined.

3. Chill until firm enough to roll into balls, about 1 hour. Preheat oven to 350°F (175°C). Form into 2 dozen balls. Press each into a lined muffin cup, leaving a deep indentation for the filling. If your tin holds only a dozen, cover extra pastry balls and return to the refrigerator.

4. For the filling: Beat sugar, egg, and vanilla with an electric mixer until smooth, scraping down bowl to make sure they are well combined. Using a rubber spatula, mix in chopped pecans until thoroughly combined.

5. To assemble: Fill each tartlet with a teaspoonful of the pecan filling and top with a pecan half.

6. Bake on middle rack of oven, 20 to 25 minutes, until set. Let cool 5 to 10 minutes, then remove from pan and transfer to cooling rack and bake remaining pastry and filling. Cool completely before storing.

BUTTER COINS

Though it seems incredible today, butter was looked on by ancient Romans as food fit only for barbarians—best suited to fuel lamps. The substance was prone to spoiling in warm climates, and only in India, where clarified butter was successfully preserved, did it become a commonplace food. It was northern Europeans, hundreds of years later, who developed and used butter as we know it today, and as milled grain became widely available, they incorporated it in their baking. In Scandinavia especially, butter cookies became a standard treat, a tradition that can still be seen in the tins

Opposite: Ginger Cookies, page 118

of Danish butter cookies and Swedish and Norwegian spritz that appear in stores at Christmas. The trouble with homemade butter cookies is that the dough is very soft and often difficult to work with. This recipe bypasses the fuss of shaping while delivering the buttery flavor of the holidays.

Makes 3 to 4 dozen cookies depending on thickness

INGREDIENTS

1 cup (225 g) unsalted butter, at room temperature

⅔ cup (130 g) granulated sugar

¼ teaspoon salt

1 large egg, separated

1 tablespoon heavy cream

1 teaspoon pure vanilla extract

2 cups (255 g) all-purpose flour

1 tablespoon water

Colored sugar (optional)

HOW-TO

1. Cream butter, sugar, and salt with an electric mixer until light and fluffy, scraping down bowl to make sure all of the butter is incorporated.

2. Combine egg yolk, cream, and vanilla in a small bowl and whisk to combine. With mixer running on low, gradually add to the butter-sugar mixture.

3. Using a rubber spatula, mix in the flour by hand until thoroughly incorporated.

4. Place half of dough on a sheet of wax paper or parchment paper and form into a log. If the dough is very soft, let it stiffen in the refrigerator a few minutes before shaping. Wrap the log completely, folding ends of wax paper or parchment over. Repeat with remaining half. Chill until dough is firm enough to slice, about 1 to 2 hours. If well wrapped, dough can be stored in refrigerator for 2 to 3 days, or frozen for several weeks.

5. Meanwhile, preheat oven to 350°F (175°C).

6. Slice cookies ¼ inch (6 mm) thick and arrange on a cookie sheet lined with parchment paper, about 1 inch (2.5 cm) apart. Some people like their cookies wafer thin, in ⅛-inch (3-mm) slices. Before baking, add 1 tablespoon water to reserved egg white and brush the top of each cookie.

7. Bake 8 to 12 minutes on middle rack of oven, rotating the pan halfway through. Baking time depends on how thick the cookies have been sliced. Cookies are done when edges just begin to turn golden brown. Cool on baking sheet about 10 minutes, then transfer to a cooling rack. If more decoration is desired, sprinkle with colored sugar while warm (but not hot). Cool completely before storing.

KRINGLER

Brought to the Scandinavian countries by Christian monks in the thirteenth century, Kringler was originally a rolled dough shaped into a pretzel-like twist. As Kringler gained popularity variations proliferated, with each locality—and often each family—making its own version. Kringler arrived in America with the Danes, Swedes, and Norwegians who immigrated in the mid-nineteenth century and, while savory Kringler can still be found, most versions today are butter-rich layers flavored with nuts, raisins, currants, or fruit.

Makes about 2 dozen bars

INGREDIENTS

For the crust:
1 cup (130 g) all-purpose flour

½ cup (115 g) unsalted butter

2 tablespoons water

For the filling:
1 cup (240 ml) water

½ cup (115 g) unsalted butter

1 cup (130 g) all-purpose flour

3 large eggs

1 to 2 teaspoons almond extract, to taste

For the glaze:

1 cup (100 g) confectioners' sugar

1 tablespoon whole milk or cream

1 tablespoon unsalted butter, melted

1 teaspoon almond extract

Slivered almonds (optional)

Colored sprinkles (optional)

HOW-TO

1. Preheat oven to 350° (175°C).

2. For the crust: Pulse all ingredients in food processor or cut with two knives as you would pie dough to make a crumbly dough that will stick together if you press it.

3. Divide dough in two balls. On a cookie sheet lined with parchment paper, pat each ball of the dough into a strip measuring about 4 by 12 inches (10 by 30.5 cm) each. The dough will be somewhat crumbly and the edges may not look neat. This is not a problem.

4. For the filling: Over medium heat, heat water and butter in a saucepan to melt butter, then increase heat to high, bring to boil, and remove from heat immediately. Add flour and stir with a heatproof rubber spatula until smooth.

5. Whisk in one egg at a time until incorporated. Add almond extract and whisk again. Spread equal amounts of filling over each strip of crust, spreading all the way to the edge.

6. Bake 35 to 40 minutes on middle rack of oven, until edges of the crust turn golden brown.

7. Remove from oven and transfer to a cooling rack. Let strips cool completely before glazing.

8. For the glaze: In a small bowl, whisk all ingredients for glaze but almonds and sprinkles until smooth. Drizzle over Kringler.

9. Garnish with slivered almonds or colored sprinkles. Slice crosswise in strips about 1 inch (2.5 cm) wide. Store leftover pastry in a cardboard box rather than a plastic container to preserve the crisp crust.

DATE BARS

Recipes using oatmeal and dried fruits like raisins and dates were especially popular during the Great Depression, quite possibly because oatmeal partially replaced more expensive flour and the sweetness of dried fruits made it possible to cut back on sugar. What we know today as classic Date Bars debuted in the early 1930s under a trio of other names—Date Sandwich Cake, Date Squares, and Matrimony Cake. According to food historians, the "Matrimony" or "Matrimonial" name was meant to describe the rough and smooth aspects of married life. By the 1950s, Date Bars had become the established name, and the treats were a popular cookie exchange and bake sale item because they were easy to prepare and transport.

Makes 16 to 20 squares

For the filling:

1½ cups (345 g) chopped, pitted dates

1 tablespoon light brown sugar

¾ cup (180 ml) water

For the crumb topping:

1 cup (130 g) all-purpose flour

½ teaspoon baking soda

Pinch of salt

1 cup (225 g) cold unsalted butter, cut in pieces

1 cup (220 g) lightly packed light brown sugar

2 cups (320 g) old-fashioned rolled oats (not quick-cooking or instant)

HOW-TO

1. Preheat oven to 350°F (175°C).

2. Combine all filling ingredients in a saucepan. Bring to a gentle boil over medium-high heat and simmer until the dates are soft enough to mash with a fork and the mixture reduces to the consistency of jam. Set aside to cool.

3. For the crumb: Pulse flour, baking soda, and salt in a food processor or whisk together in a large bowl.

4. Add butter pieces and pulse until crumbly or cut in by hand, as you would for pie crust.

5. Using a rubber spatula, mix in brown sugar and oats until incorporated.

6. Grease an 8- or 9-inch (20- or 23-cm) square baking pan and press half the crumb mixture into the bottom.

7. Spread cooled date mixture evenly over the crust, then sprinkle remaining crumb mixture over filling and press down lightly.

8. Bake 30 to 40 minutes on middle rack of oven, until crumb topping is light golden brown. Cool completely before cutting.

THUMBPRINTS

Also known as Polish Tea Cakes, Thumbprint cookies can be traced back at least two hundred years and were probably made even before that. Early European versions used almond paste as filling, as well as cooked fruits and preserves. Jam is still the most popular filling choice, though chocolate, caramel, hazelnut spread, and other candylike fillings are also common. Thumbprints have long been a favorite at cookie exchanges because they are easy to make and extremely versatile—any dough that does not spread during baking can be used, and the same basic cookie can easily be varied by using different fillings and adding a sprinkle of nuts or coconut.

Makes about 3 dozen cookies

INGREDIENTS

1 cup (225 g) unsalted butter, at room temperature

½ cup (100 g) granulated sugar

1 teaspoon pure vanilla extract

2 large eggs, separated

2 cups (255 g) all-purpose flour

Pinch of salt

2 tablespoons water (optional)

Coatings, such as finely chopped nuts or shredded sweetened coconut (optional)

Fillings such as apricot or raspberry jam, lemon curd, chocolate, or peppermint-flavored ganache

HOW-TO

1. Cream butter, sugar, and vanilla with an electric mixer until light and fluffy, scraping down bowl with a rubber spatula to make sure all of the butter is incorporated.

2. Add egg yolks and mix until combined. Mix in flour and salt until just combined. Scrape down sides of bowl again and give a final stir to make sure all of the flour has been incorporated.

3. Chill dough until firm enough to roll into 1-inch (2.5-cm) balls, about 1 hour. Once chilled and shaped, preheat oven to 350°F (175°C). Place balls 1½ inches (4 cm) apart on a cookie sheet lined with parchment paper. Gently press thumb in each cookie to make an indentation for the filling. If you want to add coatings, whisk 2 tablespoons of water into reserved egg whites, brush onto sides of cookie, and sprinkle with nuts or coconut. If you do not want to add coatings, use the whites to make Macaroons on page 120.

4. Bake on middle rack of oven for about 10 minutes, then remove from oven and fill cookies. Use a small melon baller to re-create the indentations if needed.

5. Rotate pan and return to oven for about 10 to 12 minutes, baking just until the cookies are set. Cool for 10 minutes, then transfer to cooling rack. Let cookies cool completely before storing.

DATE CAKES

The original recipe for this calls for "oleo" (margarine) rather than butter, and the use of that archaic word and the scant amount involved suggests the recipe may go back to the 1940s, when margarine first became widely used. Though available since before the turn of the century, it was disdained by most home cooks throughout the Depression. In an attempt to protect the dairy industry, many states either banned its sale, heavily taxed it, or mandated that it not be artificially colored but be sold in its natural, lard-white hue. Wartime shortages and ad campaigns emphasizing its low cost and health benefits made margarine more acceptable, though as late as the 1950s it was sold with a yellow color capsule consumers had to work into the substance themselves, and dairy states like Minnesota and Wisconsin banned its sale until the early 1960s.

Makes 4 dozen cakes
For this recipe you will need a mini muffin tin and paper liners.

INGREDIENTS

1 cup (225 g) chopped, pitted dates

1 teaspoon baking soda

1 cup (240 ml) boiling water

2 tablespoons (29 g) unsalted butter, at room temperature

1 cup (200 g) granulated sugar

1 large egg

1 teaspoon pure vanilla extract

½ cup (55 g) chopped pecans (optional)

1½ cups (170 g) all-purpose flour

1 teaspoon salt

Maraschino cherries, for garnish

1. Preheat oven to 350°F (175°C).

2. Place chopped dates in a heatproof bowl. Sprinkle with baking soda, cover with the cup of boiling water, and set aside to cool.

3. Cream butter and sugar with an electric mixer until smooth, scraping down bowl to make sure all of the butter is incorporated.

4. Add egg and vanilla and continue beating until light and fluffy.

5. Mix in cooled date mixture until combined. Then add nuts, if using, and mix again until incorporated.

6. Add flour and salt and mix until just combined.

7. Fill lined muffin cups half full and bake on middle rack of oven for 12 to 18 minutes. While still slightly warm, garnish the top of each cake with a half of a maraschino cherry. Cool completely before storing.

CHOCOLATE SOUR CREAM DROPS

Sour cream drop cookies go way back in time, to a frugal, use-it-up era when soured cream was never thrown away but rather stored in a crock in a cool basement and used to enrich other dishes. It became a key ingredient in many Russian dishes and worked its way west, eventually landing in America with European immigrants. It's probable that home bakers used sour cream in recipes that called for regular cream and liked the added tang so much that it became a featured flavor. Sugar cookie–style sour cream drops were popular in America at least a hundred years ago, and over the decades variations that included sour cream were seen in classic cookies such as oatmeal raisin, spice, shortbread, and chocolate. These cookies surfaced in the late 1950s or very early '60s and became an instant special-occasion treat. In researching this particular recipe, we have found many recipes for Chocolate Sour Cream Drops, but none that includes the magic trifecta of chocolate, coffee, and brown sugar, as this does. While commercially available sour cream can be used, nothing beats the slightly bitter, walnut-like taste of cream that has soured naturally.

Makes about 4 dozen drops

INGREDIENTS

For the cookies:

2 ounces (55 g) unsweetened chocolate, or 6 tablespoons (30 g) unsweetened cocoa powder mixed with 2 tablespoons melted unsalted butter)

¼ cup (60 ml) very strong brewed coffee

½ cup (115 g) unsalted butter, at room temperature

1 cup (220 g) packed light brown sugar

1 large egg, lightly beaten

2 cups (255 g) all-purpose flour

½ teaspoon baking soda

½ teaspoon salt

½ cup (120 ml) sour cream

For the frosting:

¼ cup (55 g) unsalted butter, softened

1 ounce (28 g) unsweetened chocolate, or 3 tablespoons unsweetened cocoa powder and 1 tablespoon melted unsalted butter

1 cup (100 g) confectioners' sugar

A few drops of whole milk, as needed

1. Preheat oven to 350°F (175°C).

2. For the cookies: In a saucepan over low heat, melt chocolate in coffee, stirring to combine, then set aside to cool.

3. Cream butter and sugar with an electric mixer until light and fluffy, scraping down bowl to make sure all of the butter is incorporated.

4. Whisk egg into cooled coffee and chocolate mixture. Add to creamed sugar and butter and mix well.

5. In a medium-sized bowl, whisk the dry ingredients together and add to the chocolate mixture alternately with the sour cream, beginning and ending with dry ingredients.

6. Drop by rounded spoonfuls onto cookie sheet lined with a silicone baking mat or parchment paper.

7. Bake on middle rack of oven just until centers are set, about 10 minutes. Let cool slightly, then transfer to cooling rack.

8. For the frosting: Cream butter with an electric mixer until light and fluffy.

9. Melt the chocolate in a small saucepan over medium-low heat and gradually add to the butter, mixing until combined.

10. Gradually add sugar, beating until frosting is smooth and satiny. If the frosting seems too stiff, thin with a few drops of whole milk.

11. Spread a thin layer of frosting over cookies while they are still warm. Cool completely before storing.

VARIATION

For a special holiday touch, flavor the frosting with a few drops of peppermint extract, or sprinkle frosted cookies with chopped nuts or bits of crushed candy cane.

SANTA'S WHISKERS

As cookie swaps became a growing trend, newspapers and magazines obliged their readers by offering torrents of ever more innovative and eye-catching cookie recipes. From cheese balls shaped like pinecones to cookies shaped like reindeer heads, those December issues of the 1960s were a winter wonderland for hostesses everywhere. Santa's Whiskers date from this era and whimsically echo Santa's jolliest features—his abundant white whiskers and cherry-red nose.

Makes about 5 dozen cookies, depending on thickness

INGREDIENTS

1 cup (225 g) unsalted butter, at room temperature

1 cup (200 g) granulated sugar

2 tablespoons whole milk

1 teaspoon pure vanilla extract

2½ cups (315 g) all-purpose flour

1 cup (155 g) drained, chopped maraschino cherries

½ cup (55 g) chopped pecans

1 cup (90 g) flaked sweetened coconut

DIRECTIONS

1. Cream butter and sugar with an electric mixer until light and fluffy, scraping down bowl to make sure all of butter is incorporated. Add milk and vanilla and mix until incorporated.

2. Add flour and mix until just combined.

3. With a rubber spatula, stir in cherries, pecans, and coconut.

4. Form dough into two 8-inch (20-cm) long logs, round or rectangular. Wrap each log in waxed paper and chill overnight.

5. Preheat oven to 350°F (175°C). Cut dough into ¼-inch-(6 mm) thick slices and arrange on a baking sheet, leaving about 1 inch (2.5 cm) of space between cookies. Bake on middle rack of oven until cookie is set and edges just begin to lightly brown, about 12 minutes. Cool completely before storing.

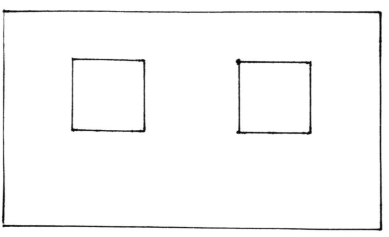

Little Village House, page 9

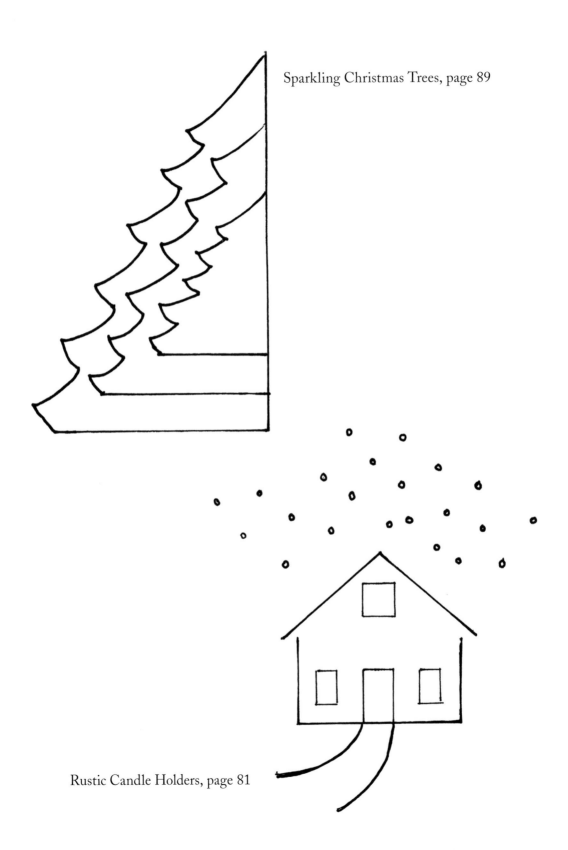

Sparkling Christmas Trees, page 89

Rustic Candle Holders, page 81

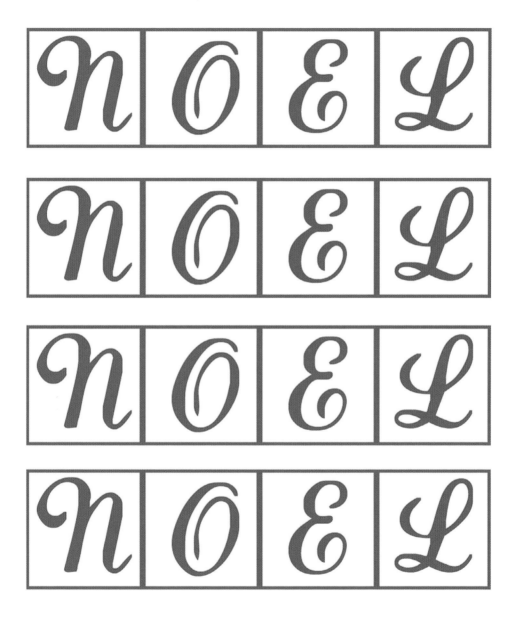

Noel Blocks, page 61

Santa Napkins, page 65

Sources